THE
JOURNEY

THE JOURNEY

Adam Thurling

RAVENSOUND
PUBLISHING

Copyright © 2022 Adam Thurling

All rights reserved. No part of this publication may be reproduced, distributed, or transmitted in any form or by any means, without prior written permission of the author.

The moral rights of the author have been asserted.

All works published by contributing authors are published with consent.

Author email: thurling@gmail.com

Ravensound Pubilshing
Brisbane, QLD, Australia

Cover Illustration & Typesetting: David Tensen

Edited: Susie Harrison & Adam Thurling

The Journey / Adam Thurling 2022
ISBN 978-0-6489893-3-2

*Dedicated to Jess
and my boys.*

ENDORSEMENTS

I first had the privilege of meeting Adam some 15 or so years ago when we were pastoring in Adelaide. I immediately took a liking to him as I saw some characteristics in him that reminded me a great deal of myself. He had a cheeky larrikin personality accompanied by a huge passion to know and serve God. He was still working through traumas and scars from his traumatic past but passionately setting himself to make a big mark for God.

This book, *The Journey*, is brutally honest and challenging. It gives a great picture of the Father's love coming to cleanse and defuse the pain of the past and to build a strength of character that in Robert Schuller's words, "turns our scars into stars".

Today, Adam is a powerful man of God in full time ministry. A loving husband and a doting father. His journey will inspire and motivate you to grow in God's love and enthusiastically embrace the journey and totally fulfil your destiny.

Tim Hall - Director - Tim Hall International Ministries

If Christianity has been hijacked by a culture of fear, guilt and condemnation, Adam Thurlings book is like a SWAT team smashing through the windows of our deceit and eliminating the lies that are holding us hostage. Through inspiring stories and deep revelation Adam Thurling takes you on a journey into the heart of God where there is more truth, freedom and restoration than you had ever imagined!

James Thompson - Network Pastor City Life - Casey

Adam has spent countless hours wrestling with the heart of God and the many issues faced within church culture, so I am thrilled that he has taken the time to not only document his story, but also the many revelations and convictions he's had along the way. It's my prayer that those who read this book would come to know the same incredible heart Adam has for God that I've seen first hand and most importantly, fall more in love with our wonderful Jesus.

James Mitchell - Friend

The story of how Adam met God in a park in South Australia is reason enough to read this book. The "meat" however, is in the radical transformation that ensues. Adam Thurling takes readers on his very personal journey of meeting God to accepting himself to challenging misconceptions about God that many Christians (and non-Christians) have been led to believe. For anyone skeptical about God's love, skeptical that God is actually good, then this is a must read and a journey not to be missed.

Jono Newmarch - Itinerate Minister

I have had the privilege of working alongside Adam for the last 4 years and I have seen the fruit of his ministry first hand. He is anointed to bring the good news; that which sets people free by the work of Christ, not by the work of man.

He is a man of integrity and deep conviction, whilst his commitment to processing his journey in life through the lens of a loving Heavenly Father is inspiring.

Adam's life is evidence of the redemptive power of Jesus. This book is filled with examples and revelations of what partnering with God's word and promise does for any willing person.

Adam has been transformed by God's love, grace and power and through these words you will also be challenged and encouraged to live the transformed life by Christ.

Andrew Newman - Senior Leader - Eternity Church Morwell

FOREWORD

I believe that no two paths to God are textured by the same terrain. Instead, our absolute uniqueness must be taken into account when considering how God is discovered, uncovered and recovered across the landscape of our lives.

If you have faith to accept that you are unique and special, you also must accept that you will remain what Rabbi Joseph B. Soloveitchik calls *A lonely person of faith*. Why? Because if you accept that you are so incredibly unique, you *cannot* expect anyone else on the face of the earth to really understand you. Not a parent. Not a partner. Not even yourself.

Yet, so many of us long to be known in the hope that we might truly come to know ourselves. I would argue that this longing draws so many of us towards spirituality and religion. We long to be good or worthy or accepted or, dare I say it, loved.

The problem with a lot of messaging in books, sermons and theology created to deliver us from this longing is they lack two things; *heart* and *patience*. Thankfully, Adam's work has both heart and patience in abundance.

Heart, to me, speaks of sincere and unmasked storytelling. Heart dares attach meaning to failure. Heart shines a torch of hope against a dark past. Heart even finds a way to apply an ancient text to modern personhood. You will find yourself moving across these aspects in this book. Adam manages to do this by tearing off the bread of his own life and generously sharing it with the reader.

When we move beyond patience being something tested in traffic, patience becomes a virtue best imparted through another's experience. I'm so glad Adam has written the arc of this book with a never-ending story in mind. A story which, for me personally, is still unfolding and will likely continue to be told past my final breath. *It is the story of a divine eternal family.* It is a story which we are all part of - whether or not we chose to see God as a father, friend, lover or judge.

I invite you, along with Adam, to not just see the author's story in these pages, but grant yourself the permission to consider God, yourself and the world in light of the outrageous Love which fills so many of these pages.

As someone who has had the great privilege of being a mentor, and now a good friend of the author, I wholeheartedly pray this book finds you exactly where you are today and inspires you to walk towards the journey of accepting who you really are above all else; beloved.

David Tensen - Author, poet, friend.

The Journey

Table of Contents

INTRODUCTION *1*

THE OUTWORKING *9*

MAKE YOUR TRIALS WORTH IT *15*

THE STORY OF THE FATHER'S PURSUIT *29*

THE STORY OF OUR FATHER'S PURSUIT CONTINUED IN INTIMACY. *47*

THE STORY IN THE LIE OF UNWORTHINESS *67*

THE STORY OF THE FATHER'S NATURE *83*

THE STORY OF JUDGMENT *97*

THE STORY OF FRIENDSHIP..................................... *115*

THE STORY OF UNDERSTANDING LOVE *132*

THE STORY OF TENSION BETWEEN GRACE AND TRUTH *149*

THE STORY OF THE GOSPEL *173*

INTRODUCTION

Think of this book as an invitation. I want you to share my journey and the revelations I've received and explored over the years. These revelations have led me into the heart of God. I will share my Story with you and invite you into my journey of knowing the Father and being known by Him in return. My thoughts and beliefs continue to be formed by these experiences of His kindness in my life; I want to provoke in you the same desire to begin to know Him deeply in the expression of your journey. I will lay my experiences at your feet to inspire you to be courageous and curious in your relational journey with God. These experiences have shaped my faith with God, they have been formed in many different ways, both in personal moments of intimate revelations and in public moments of discovery of his intent for others. They have also been formed through visions and dreams and most importantly, journeying through my pain. Perhaps the most powerful transformation has come through reconciling these experiences with scripture and finding the truth of God and His heart for us within.

Let me explain.

I mean that often I have found myself in conversations or moments that at some point, I begin to sense a profound expression of a need or a pain that I sense God wants to shift in my life or if in connection to others, their heart.

It's as if I hear God say, "they're hurting," or "they're stuck." When God reveals the problem, it's like turning a key sitting in a keyhole that's never clicked open. It often feels like I see someone standing at a door that they have never opened before. Helping them turn the key usually seems like ushering in value statements, a corrective word, or a message of change in their lives by partnering with the Father's intent to bring an area of transformation. This could range from correcting personal value statements or simply a new revelation of God's nature and anything in between.

I get to see the person or even myself through the eyes of God in these moments, I often get the privilege of feeling their pain. As we converse, it seems as though the Father is giving me the language to speak with their Spirit to bring life.

Let me give an example. I was sharing at a young adult meeting a few years back, I sensed feelings of anticipation attached to a sense of sorrow that seemed to be connected with this girl. I started speaking to her about the Father desiring to give her a gift and that it would come within three weeks. As I explored this display of God's heart toward her, she revealed that her birthday was in three weeks and that her parents had never really celebrated with her. The Father wanted to redeem this for her by giving her a gift on her birthday. I still shake my head at this reality. Months later I learned that she was getting engaged to the man of her dreams and she had met him, you guessed it, on her birthday!

This is one of many instances that the Father has redeemed someone and restored an area of their life through a feeling of empathy towards someone's pain. Insights like these are commonplace when dealing with an intentional God of love; often, He surrounds areas of our lives without our awareness and is purposeful in His pursuit for change in our lives.

In many of these experiences of the Father's heart towards people, I am left perplexed by the overflow of His intent which provokes change in me. Often, I have left a conversation feeling challenged in my own thoughts of His intention to bring a deeper change in me. I would find myself left in a place of searching, and often it brought me into a deeper insight of love that would also unlock new insights for my own life. What I experienced through these expressions of God's heart for people would become a catalyst for my exploration of His intention toward me. These moments would begin to solidify further my experience that one of the primary ways to explore the heart of God is to be intrinsically connected to other believers and live deeply in community.

During these time's in my life, the Spirit would often lead me to scripture to back up and confirm the experiences that contradicted my value system. Unfortunately, I didn't necessarily understand or allow these realities to be applied to my own life. I would fail to see that these expressions toward me from God and through me to people were more of an invitation than an expression of my success as a Christian. It upsets me to admit I often wore them as a badge of honour instead of seeking the invitation that God was offering; "Adam, this is how I want to love you."

I have found Him to be a God who loves us enough to sometimes collide with our religious views and set us free from what we thought was freedom. Occasionally, we need to drop our perceptions of truth to allow a shift in our perspective of it. We learn what true freedom looks like in a deep relationship with God, but sometimes what we have learned is at odds with what we have experienced.

As humans, we often fail to offer ourselves the same grace and freedom that we offer others. But why? Because we know the depravity of our hearts and the desire we have for freedom, we don't often believe what we have experienced can go beyond how we feel about ourselves. So, we put our beliefs and value systems in the hands of men who teach about God instead of God himself; we allow our definition of the God we have met to be shaped by man's views.

On the flip side of this, when we have a belief set that isn't tuned into a loving and kind God when approached with someone's mess, we often offer how we believe we deserve to be viewed in God's eyes instead of showing true grace. It is usually due to our struggle; in these moments, we express something other than the heart of God. Our expression becomes our reality instead of truth. Laying in my subconscious, at least, was a desire to see someone else struggle deeper than me with love to elevate the shame I felt in day-to-day life.

Through this, my expression of "grace" is dictated by the terms of my ability to accept its truth in my own life, and on any given day, my extension of grace could be different based on what I was thinking or feeling about myself. This has taught me that understanding God simply was not enough; instead, to be known by Him had to be the answer.

Because of this, what we express to others concerning the revelation of the love of the Father, we struggle to reconcile in ourselves. This inability to extend what we believe about love beyond our borders does perpetual damage to those we walk with. As I stated earlier, one of the main reasons this happens is because we are more deeply aware of our own mistakes, shame and brokenness; it is far easier to extend love to someone you are external from, not knowing what they are hiding. It may be a case of "ignorance is bliss", or perhaps what it truly is could be better summarised as disconnection. As humans, we find it easy to extend grace to each other.

However, due to our ingrained shame complex, when it comes to loving ourselves well, we struggle to accept the realities of acceptance itself. For instance, we often read over definitive scriptures without applying them. We skip over verses like these very final words that Jesus utters on the cross with his final breath, "It is finished," and then go and resurrect our sin as if we have that power. We so easily extend grace to others because it is easier to believe that they are worth it, but I am here to tell you, friend, you are more than worth it - you are so loved that you, my friend, are worth dying for. Welcome to my journey in that process.

The Journey

Dedication

I want to dedicate this book to my wife, who continually champions me and helps me see my value in God's eyes through her fierce love for me. I love you, Jess, and would not be here without you and the Father. I also cannot fail to mention the countless kingdom family members who have championed me, challenged me and set me free in love through their expression of His kindness toward me. And last but not least to my sons Isaiah and Zeak. This is on paper for you and you alone. Anyone who benefits from this work benefits from your very existence. I love you, my boys.

Thank you all.
Adam

The Journey

THE OUTWORKING

Dreams, in my experience, have been a primary source in finding definitions surrounding scriptural truth. Often, I have gone to sleep and met with the Father. In these times, He has brought me to a place of more profound understanding of these experiences that make up my journey.

This would help me find scriptural definitions surrounding the growing change in my belief system. Incredibly it has helped me understand what I have experienced with Him in my day-to-day life. Later in this book, I will attempt to explore some of these with you and give you some insight. I have begun to find myself in the constant presence of a God who has loved me deeply through His desire to see His son return to the truth of His love and come home to His embrace.

We see very early on in scripture the use of dreams to interpret experience in life. As a primary example in Genesis, Joseph was sought after for his ability in interpretation and even used it in the context of evangelism while dealing with Pharaoh.

Genesis 41:15

And Pharaoh said to Joseph, "I have had a dream, and there is no one who can interpret it. I have heard it said of you that when you hear a dream, you can interpret it."

If we were looking for two or three instances where dreams are used as a way for God to speak, we would not have to look too much further than Daniel. Here he seems to give us context surrounding God's intent through this method of communication.

Daniel 2:28

But there is a God in heaven who reveals mysteries, and he has made known to King Nebuchadnezzar what will be in the latter days. Your dream and the visions of your head as you lay in bed are these.

Through this reality, I have learnt this truth; there are mysteries that the Father wants to reveal. Your dreams offer insights into some deep secrets held within your heart between you and the Father.

Later in this book, I will explore some of the revelation moments I have had with the Father in my sleep. These have been some of the most transformational times for me.

Visions. Another way that God has revealed areas of my heart that have been locked away. Let's begin by providing some definition of what a vision is. It looks like something seen in a dream, trance, or religious ecstasy. It is a supernatural experience that, within my encounters, usually conveys some kind of revelation. After receiving a vision, I would be deeply challenged to break free from an area of my heart that has - or is - holding me back from a breakthrough of some type. Allow me to share a story with you as an example of what I am trying to express.

A few years ago, I envisioned being the prodigal son in Jesus' famous parable. I was in a church service, and I was on my knees during the worship segment before the sermon. As I knelt in front of my chair, I looked up, and a vision began; it was as if I was looking up at a cinema screen. I saw myself playing the role of the prodigal son in Jesus' parable from Luke 15. It began as I walked up a hill on a dirt path, with green grass on both sides of me. Finally, I approached the top of the mountain. From all the times I'd sat with my Father on the porch, I knew that I'd be visible when I got there. Somehow (perhaps it's a vision thing), I also knew that my Father was waiting on the porch and looking up at the hill in anxious anticipation of my return. Even as I type this, I am reminded of the emotion I felt as I sat on the hill just out of sight. At this moment, I began realising that I wasn't confident that I was ready to receive this kind of love and take that step towards being seen by my Father in my mess.

At this point in my life, I had already started the journey into something more than a mere cognitive understanding that God loves me. I think many people make it this far in the journey, but how many walk over the hill to receive the Father's love and embrace it? The gap between belief and acceptance had never been more apparent. Was I worth loving? I stopped just before coming into view at the peak of the hill. One more step, and my Father would have seen me. I sat down on the path, thinking, "Am I ready for this kind of love?" It was as if I knew that it would cost me my life and change everything. The vision stopped there. I knew I was invited into a deeper reality that I had to choose to step into.

The truths God was calling me into - not just a cognitive understanding that He loves me but also that I was, in fact, worth loving. This is an example of how God has used visions in my life.

Throughout scripture, we see that God has used this communication medium to unlock potential and provoke insight in people's lives. For instance, God's question to Saul on the road to Damascus gives us a great example of the inquisitive nature of God: "Saul, why do you persecute me?" This led to a direct question to God on Saul's behalf, "Who are you, Lord?"

Acts 9:4 (ESV)

And falling to the ground, he heard a voice saying to him, "Saul, Saul, why are you persecuting me?"

Acts 9:5

And he said, "Who are you, Lord?" And he said, "I am Jesus, whom you are persecuting."

When we pay attention to the details of this encounter, we see a God who is intentionally seeking a man who has talent and anointing, operating in a false calling. What I mean by this statement is this: the gifts of God know no repentance (Romans 11:29). This means we can operate in our anointing outside of God's will in our lives. As an anointed leader and perfect teacher of the law, Saul worked in gifts God had given him outside of a relationship. So, in this instance, God decides to collide with Saul's direction in life. He meets with Saul and invites him into a conversation surrounding understanding. I have had many experiences like this where the Father has intervened on my journey with questions that are veiled in curiosity. Although, he is a very kind and gentle God; through these kinds of experiences with Him, I have learnt that his curiosity is an invitation to deeper relational conversation.

The journey of pain has been a way to learn about God and His goodness. The process of reconciling to a God who loves us relentlessly amid rejection, failure, and disappointment has led me to some of the most profound revelatory insights I have experienced. Within our pain lies an opportunity; this is the potential discovery of another facet of His nature that is the desire to reveal himself as not only a God who heals but also one that has intentions toward restoration. He desires to heal and restore to us through a discovery of truth surrounding our experiences, and if we let them, these wounds will lead us to a new reality surrounding our pain. In these moments, we have an opportunity to lean deeper into his heart for us, or we can miss His intentional use of the situation that presents itself.

Jesus is the foundation that we have set ourselves upon, and He continues to be steadfast in love for us all. Thank you for taking the time to become a part of my journey and my world. I firmly believe in you even if we haven't met. I believe in your life's destiny and the person you are as much as the one you will become.

The Journey

MAKE YOUR TRIALS WORTH IT

I can recall a moment I had a few years back while worshiping at an Atlas gathering in Melbourne. I remember it so clearly: it felt like a tangible embrace of the Father's heart. I had just had a conversation with a friend before our service about trials and how we could find God in them. Had I stayed aware that He was listening and was currently implementing this into my life, I may have been able to offer some better advice to my friend. It is as if I can feel it now as I type, a tangible embrace followed by a faint whisper. So this is what He said to me, "Adam, make your trials worth it."

Throughout this chapter, I will try to establish some realities surrounding God and our trials. This is purely to lay a foundation of God's love and His involvement in the pain of our lives. However, before we begin, I want to say that there is much room for you to take offense in a few following thoughts. My intention is not to offer you an opportunity toward offense, that is not what is on offer here, but it is what you can take.

I urge you to read through the challenging ideas and consider them with God while remembering that this is an invitation into my process with the Lord. To be clear, what I am not offering here is a definitive conclusion on any topic that follows; I believe that your journey of faith is entirely your own. You must discover your relational reality with God.

No one has the right - including me - to tell you how to walk out your faith in God or your relationship with Him. To help you move forward in your growth, I urge you to become comfortable with differences and disagreements and grow within them. Be relational in it; embrace thoughts that challenge to the core what you believe and have learnt through tradition instead of discovery.

In the West, we have a sickness attached to our faith. It is the behaviour we call arrogance, and I want to offer you a remedy for this throughout these pages.

In our limited one-dimensional language, we believe that we are the final authority on this exhaustive document, the Bible, which is expressed in a language designed to paint images of God's character with broad strokes instead of defining him right down to the correct full stop. We, in the West, love to define God; however, they have mastered the art of discovering him in the East.

In the West, we believe it essential to offer definitive conclusions on what the Bible labels as mysteries. In the East, the book is an invitation to go on a journey to discover the ever-deepening secret of who God is.

Perhaps a great example of the differences we have in our approach to God from an eastern perspective to a western one could be the art of connection in disagreement. In the West, we argue until we have a definition around our thoughts; we theorise God and theology and then box God into our realities. In the East, we are invited into a discourse surrounding the discovery that God is far more relational, and He is presented that way. This is something the Eastern church has over us in the West. It is something we need to learn.

Before I heard these words in my Spirit, "Make your trials worth it," I would look at my trials and disagreements as an issue to solve instead of a tension to hold. This mindset led me to move through some profound revelations without paying them the attention they deserved. You have to understand; that if we don't look at who God is in the most challenging areas of our lives, we will miss something so transformative and powerful. The trial has a profound lesson to teach you.

Unfortunately, we often neglect to invite God into these spaces. I did this subconsciously through fear of being proven wrong in my beliefs earlier in my journey. If I ask God in, He will either prove me right that he is absent and uncaring or prove me wrong and pull me deeper into a relationship that will cost me my life. These thoughts were a lie; they didn't cost me my life. What I had could not be called life compared to what I now have in Him. We are taught misconceptions about God birthed in the fear and insecurities of those we look up to. It is not intentional, and it is not evil; it is simply human.

So what was God trying to say to me?

I don't know how people walk through life without the reality of God's presence. Personally, until this point in my life, including the space I am in right now, I have walked through a multitude of pain in my world while learning how to embrace it without allowing it to define me. It is a testimony that I can stand before our God and trust that He is good.

Honestly, it was not too long ago in the past that I was crippled by confused thoughts surrounding His character when trying to reconcile some of what I experienced.

This confusion embedded itself in what was lying in the subconscious of my thoughts and not in the outworking of my faith. I seemed to be able to function during the confusion and a lack of trust. In the areas where I found mistrust, I thankfully found a helpful curiosity about His nature.

Questions slowly surfaced that I almost felt bad for asking. They sounded like this: "If He is so good, then why did all of this happen to me?" Later in this book, I intend to delve into this, but for now, I would like to focus on what I learned in making the reality of my trials worth it.

The current stand I take surrounding pain and trial is that how we respond to it will forge our future path. If we stay in it and focus on all the things we can blame for our state of mind or attitude, the direction will remain unclear and pointless.

However, before I understood the Father's heart, I would often react to pain instead of respond. The reaction would always look like controlling the situation and making sure it was contained, I would attempt to create a situation in which I felt safe, while responding always seemed to end up looking like resting and trusting the intention of God during the conflict.

This process of living in response to trials instead of reaction is a portion of what we are called to do as God's people. We see this modelled in Paul's life.

Acts 14:22

strengthening the souls of the disciples, encouraging them to continue in the faith, and saying that through many tribulations, we must enter the kingdom of God.

It is a challenging truth for me that Paul spoke this sentence directly after being stoned by the Jewish followers in Antioch. They had dragged him out of the city, "supposing he was dead." This was a brutal attack and a near-death experience, but his response should stun us. The next day, he goes back into the city, begins preaching with Barnabas, and successfully makes some more disciples. He then leaves and utters such an intensely stressful bottom line. He says this: "Through many trials and tribulations, we must enter the kingdom of God." This seems in scripture to look like walking in the empowerment of grace through trial instead of using wisdom to avoid it.

We see him say again later in 2 Timothy 1:8, "Endure all sufferings, do the work of an evangelist and fulfill your ministry." There is a potential fear in this relational reality that could play out. It does not sound like fun to be in a relationship with suffering through Christ. However, we don't see fear rise up in Timothy. Why?

Here Paul has finished telling Timothy that if he chooses to continue in his faith journey. "Timothy, follow me as I follow Christ, and following Christ means suffering." It is as if Paul is pointing to his scars in this text: "I have the scars to prove it." It is in Paul's empowerment through grace that Timothy stays focused. He sees that Christ is with Paul and that the grace in his life has empowered him to see the trials for their benefit. Instead of looking at the reality that these things are hard, he looks directly at the fruit and can't wait to have the same freedom on display. I would personally love to have Paul's impact.

Therefore, I choose to embrace the pain in my life instead of running from it. I decided to understand it rather than trying to deny it.

Isaiah 55:8

My thoughts are not your thoughts, neither are your ways, my ways, saith Jehovah.

In trials, we need to trust in His character. Having this wrong will take us into a warped view. This leads to a misinterpretation of what is happening in our lives.

So let's look at making our trials worth it.

James 1:2

Count it all joy, my brothers, when you meet trials of various kinds.

The first thing we need to do is count it as joy! Now, this does not mean ignoring, pretending and looking happy until it passes. Instead, it means a profound joy that surpasses our desire to understand, and this is rooted in the trust in whom He has revealed Himself to be.

Through a shame-filled culture, we have learnt to devalue how we feel and not burden each other with our issues. In church, we smile and raise our hands through our trials and when asked, "How are you going?" We brush any reality to the side with a simple one-word answer, "good." This is detrimental to our mental, physical and emotional health and keeps us hidden from our peers.

However, if this is taught well, "the idea of counting our trials as joy" means sustained peace instead of momentary happiness. There is truth and power in our response to trials while doing it in authenticity. I would encourage you to journey and process with your peers, but let's make sure we end our processing in joy to respond to God's goodness in the journey.

Paul's response was honest, vulnerable and authentic in the face of trials, but we need to understand that there is something special about not hiding in these realities. I know that in my life, I used these actions to hide my actual situation to disarm people who were trying to care for me; I would give them what they wanted, so they didn't ask any further questions. Paul lent in toward the testimony of his response to speak of who God was to him.

We can answer honestly and struggle while still walking in joy. You see, joy and happiness are two different things. Happiness is defined as a moment of exultation, and joy throughout scripture is a steadfast strength to endure.

As Jesus in the garden prayed, as recorded in the book of Hebrews in chapter twelve, verses 1-2, "But for the JOY set before me I will endure." I can not imagine this being an overly happy moment for Jesus, but it was His strength in the joy of the accomplished goal to do the Father's will that sustained the path he had to take.

Acts 20:19

serving the Lord with all humility and with tears and with trials that happened to me through the plots of the Jews;

James 1:3

for you know that the testing of your faith produces steadfastness.

We need to push through in our trials, friends. It is so important to do this because it provides growth for us. When we have a correct view of God's heart during our battles, we can endure difficult and complicated circumstances with strength and self-control. This understanding of God's heart will produce the ability and the will to survive anything that the world can throw our way with power and grace. This creates a desire to hold fast to the God we love instead of idolising the God of our circumstances. When it comes to God and our trial, we often draw on conclusions of fantasy about Him while enduring our circumstances.

God is no magician. However, I have experienced moments of freedom from pain instantly in my life. Unfortunately, it is not always the case. We need to be careful about our trials' language because this whole one-stop-shop consumer Christianity disempowers people on an authentic journey to freedom. Let's look at what it says in James, for example.

James 1:4

and let steadfastness have its full effect that you may be perfect and complete, lacking in nothing.

When we disempower the journey with magical faith statements, we can destroy the process someone is going through. We begin to deconstruct what God is trying to build through a steadfastness that can only be completed in a trial. We need to understand that trial has the purpose of creating a full effect on people. Often, we can step into the place of saviour and forget what built the strength in us in the first instance. The trial makes us perfect and complete, lacking in nothing. In this area, I would encourage you to take the words of James seriously in your pursuit of freedom. If you are chasing a moment that will set you free while God is trying to do a work in progress, you will become gravely disappointed and often left in despair about the nature of the God you serve.

Ask the Father, what do you want from me in this situation? Are we on a journey, or should I press in for a miracle? Both realities are valid, and what I am presenting here is a holistic view of our journeys. So often, there is no middle ground, and we focus on either a miracle or a process.

James 1:5

If any of you lacks wisdom, let him ask God, who gives generously to all without reproach, and it will be given to him.

We need to be transparent with God, asking for wisdom and understanding when we lack it, knowing that He is not the author of our trials. He will turn the work of the enemy into something special. God will only achieve this in a healthy response to His character from within our test.

So again, I hear the question, "How do we make our trials worth it?" I believe it is in praise and the process of counting all trials a joy. Stand in His presence, and the result is simple. It is not actually about your victory: it is about the relationship you carry with God on the way to the outcome. We love to make it about us, and what God has achieved in us is often our praise point, but it is actually about who we are with Him in the journey, and the outcome will take care of itself.

So, as you journey with me through this book, I would ask you to open your heart up to the process that the Father is inviting you into. Through some of the insights I will share with you here, there will be many moments when you could feel uncertain about what I have to say. By no means do I believe that I have the complete picture. I am still going through spiritual growing pains that are teaching me great lessons that, one day, I hope to share with you. My intention is not to offer definitive thought, although as it stands right now, this is where I sit about some theological statements. Instead, I hope that I will be able to provoke dialogue between you and my loving Father that will bring a more profound sense of freedom into your life.

At the beginning of each chapter, I will share the encounter, dream, vision, or pain as a story. These moments were the catalyst for the thought or revelation that I will present. I intend on inviting you on the intimate process that I journey through with the Father, in pain and joy, freedom and bondage, breakthrough and breaking. I intend to share with you, in reality, the vulnerability it takes to walk this out in community and intimacy.

So let me pray for you this simple yet powerful prayer as we agree that this will be a time and a moment when God will answer the most profound parts of your heart and that you would be empowered as I was, to become honest with the Father. So the prophecy for you is this, for those who have chosen to go on this journey:

The scripture says this in John 1:5

The light shines in the darkness, and the darkness has not overcome it.

I prophesy right now that the darkness in you will come into a perfect understanding. We need to understand that all sin is empowered by the pure lie that God does not love you amid the mess you are. In this season, I pray that you will become so aware of His divine love for you that shame will no longer hinder you. I pray that a profound revelation of love will break off guilt and self-worth issues through this.

Hold onto this scripture in Ephesians as we journey.

Ephesians 3:17-20

So that Christ may dwell in your hearts through faith - that you, being rooted and grounded in love, may have the strength to comprehend with all the saints what are the breadth and length and height and depth, and to know the love of Christ that surpasses knowledge that you may be filled with all the fullness of God.

"With all the fullness of God." There is nothing partial about our God when it comes to generosity. He has given himself to you wholeheartedly. So I want to encourage you today to sit in the reality of that place and read on from that position of intimate belonging.

I imagine us all as the sinners resting on the chest of Jesus as He ate at the tax collectors' house. He wants us to know these simple words: "I desire mercy, not sacrifice!"

Hebrews 12:5-9

And have you forgotten the exhortation that addresses you as sons? "My son, do not regard lightly the discipline of the Lord, Nor be weary when reproved by him. For the Lord disciplines the one he loves, And chastises every son whom he receives."

Adam Thurling

The Journey

THE STORY OF THE FATHER'S PURSUIT

For me, real life began at the age of eighteen. In this stage of my life, I had to come to terms with the end of my natural self as I began to encounter the spiritual reality of becoming a child of God. By this point, I had walked through many trials and tried so many different avenues to alleviate the emotional pain. However, nothing that I could find in a worldly sense would result in freedom from the emotional emptiness dictating my life's terms. I was bound by a value statement that screamed from the depth of my heart, "Adam, you are the product of your mistakes; you are worth nothing!"

From the age of fifteen until my initial encounter with God, I primarily lived out of home on friend's lounge chairs and in a youth home run by Baptist Care in South Australia. This was due to my criminal and violent nature toward my family. I was not safe to be around, and I was aware of this and, in some circumstances, used it to manipulate my way into getting what I wanted. My anger at the world and my pain had finally taken its toll on what relationships I had left in the aftermath of our family unit breakdown.

Coming towards the end of this time in my life, it was a struggle to see how survival was an option. However, there came one final image of hope in the form of a family that had taken it upon themselves to try and intervene in my circumstance. They had offered me a place to stay in their home in response to my mother's situation with me. This family was a part of a local church that I interacted with through community outreach, and they were also friends with my parents during one of the most challenging times of their lives. They had indeed seen firsthand what we had to try and reconcile as children.

Heather and Steve watched me grow up and were deeply aware of the carnage that the relational breakdown between my parents had caused for me. It is incredible that somehow God connected dots to tie in Heather and Steve to my journey of transformation; knowing them for years, I had no idea they were church-going faith-filled believers. Yet incredibly, I had met their local pastor on the streets of a little suburb of South Australia called Aberfoyle Park at an outreach that fed hundreds of local teens that were out late at night. This is likely where they gained their desire to help me. Throughout the time at Heather and Steve's house, God had begun the process of grabbing my attention. I owe a lot to the safe environment they provided in that short season, but even for them, my spiral had become too much for their family home.

I remember watching them take me in while trying to understand why they felt I was worth the challenge. Heather and Steve had decided to place their children's safety at risk, and their comfort, to house me. The feeling was foreign to me, as I had typically felt alone and unwanted, but they somehow could look at me as valuable and worth helping.

Looking back, this situation was one of the catalyst moments for what would take place in my life. There are many people I wish to attribute my newfound freedom to, but this couple was the face of a God I didn't know yet, and I am deeply thankful for them for the risk they took on a violent, disruptive, and unwilling eighteen-year-old.

Before I enter into the Story of how it all changed, I want to rewind here and share one of the darkest times of my life with you. I grew up in a home that would seem to be a loving and stable environment if you were looking from the outside. But unfortunately, this was not the case.

My Dad worked hard to provide the best for us in a material sense but was not present for us in nurture and growth. In his childhood, there were wounds not unlike those given to us, and he began to repeat the cycle of alcoholism and anger that he had experienced. It was the only form of love that he knew, and as a child, I quickly began to learn it.

My mother prepared us for what was ahead each day and was a ferocious lover of her children. However, she also seemed unable to guide us into what was right and wrong and found herself exhausted by the intensity of our household on a day-to-day basis. My parents are both great people - by no means was there an intentional expression that led me to become who I became. It is the truth that we are all victims of our circumstances and need to take responsibility for our actions. It is not my intention to lay blame but instead to paint a picture of what my childhood was like from my perspective.

Undoubtedly, my parents did the best they could with their given tools. However, there was an emotional disconnection between us as children toward our parents. The wound in me was deep in my subconscious, and I began to believe I existed as a point of affirmation and nurture for my mother. Her bucket was empty, and I felt I needed to fill it. My mother's childhood was void of nurture, and as is true with anything, if you don't stop the cycle, you will repeat it. So my mother got her bucket filled up with her children's success - or failures.

She would use us without knowing it to get the attention she craved, whether negative or positive. On the other hand, my father was the son of an alcoholic who was abusive to my grandmother in front of him during his childhood. My grandmother is my hero and is one of the most forgiving women you could ever meet, but she was the victim of an abusive situation that spiraled out of control.

Being the eldest of four, my Dad was witness to many things that I only heard about in the later years of my life. It is a testament to my grandmother and my Dad's nature that I grew up with my grandfather portrayed as a hero and not a villain. As I grew and discovered more of our family history, I found this very far from the truth.

Although I had discovered truths about my grandfather that had been shocking, my memory of this man is fond. He was caring, loving, and able to be present. May the goodness I experienced be the memory and testament of a man changed throughout a tough life.

My mother is a fierce woman who can survive anything, having lived in and through an emotional and physically abusive childhood. Consequently, she was not emotionally equipped to provide the environment of nurture we needed to thrive. Instead, we survived and did this any way we possibly could.

If I am honest, the effects of my childhood have been a point of contention for me. On the one hand, I mourn with a sense of anger, and on the other, I praise God because of the people I have been able to help.

My parents are merely victims of their upbringing, which set them up to fail because they had no healthy parenting guidelines, And all too often, we perpetuate our normal. This is where I formed the grace and forgiveness I carry for them both, and as I share our story from my perspective, you must know that I consider myself lucky to have the parents I have. This is a redemptive story of a broken child who takes responsibility for his reaction to the situation. I made my own choices, which led to the lifestyle I lived, not my parents.

I sincerely wish that I had possessed the capacity, as a child, to extend grace through understanding. Perhaps if this was a reality, I might have reacted differently. But, like most children, I had no capacity for this knowledge at that age.

Throughout primary school, I began to find myself sexually active, physically violent, and verbally abusive toward other students and teachers. And here is the thing; I had no idea why.

The love between my parents was dysfunctional at best and scarcely present. However, once I began to journey through this in a healing context, I realised that the foundation of my acting out behaviour had been an effort to feel seen and feel some kind of emotional connection. Even negative attention was enough for me to feel loved. If I had not addressed this in my later life, I would have continued the cycle of abuse that generations in my family have perpetuated upon one another throughout our childhoods that we have a shared hatred of.

I believe if you were to ask my mother and Father about their childhoods, their expression and pain would be much the same as mine. Therefore, I urge you not to play the blame game but instead take responsibility for your family's future and heal yourself so that you can produce for your children a pure love.

At a very young age, my parents explored what was going on for me through this season. I was told I was a troubled child and worse. From outside of our family unit, many voices explained that I had no reason to behave the way I was. My parents had been functioning quite well in public, and no one else could see what was happening - not even my parents could. How easy it is for us to hide from the evident realities around us when our pain masks the view in which we see things.

This began a lifestyle of confusion for me. Questions like "What is wrong with me" were commonplace in my day-to-day thinking from the ripe old age of six years old, and I started to develop a profound hiddenness based on my perception of life through pain. Even as a child, I looked to myself for the answers. I never entirely felt I could understand myself, let alone feel understood by others.

The question of what was wrong with me led into deep spirals of exploration in darkness. It went from sporting highs to feeling loved, to drug highs and even exploring the potential of being gay to alleviate my emotional state. I searched high and low to feel like I could love and value myself. What was wrong with me? No one had an answer, and I had no way of even beginning the journey to finding one.

For a moment, let me explore the statement I made earlier surrounding "profound hiddenness." I need to stress that it was not in the sense of real hiding, but instead, I became louder and worked harder to be seen. I became the best at everything to receive praise and developed the need to be necessary to someone or anyone who would make me feel special. If I wasn't the best, I would lie my way into people thinking I was. So, I would go to the extreme when being naughty as at least I would briefly experience the feeling of being seen. It was there that I birthed the beginning of a religious performance lifestyle, and when I joined the church, it had the necessary attributes to feed my wounds deeply.

Once I met God, I carried this behaviour into our relationship, feeling as though it was easier to feel connection if I was remorseful for what I deemed a sin in my life. While I am here, let me say that if your version of connection to love is firmly attached to acceptance through behaviour, then it is not indeed a connection at all. Instead, you are in an abusive relationship where your view of God is your abuse of yourself. We need to take off the shades of our preconceived ideas about God when dealing with pain. If you are honest with yourself, you will realise that you have formed an opinion based on life experience in conjunction with who He is. This means you are letting your perception and experience define truth instead of allowing truth to bend those things.

I will explore that last statement more profoundly throughout this book, but I need to stress that my family was not remotely God-filled for now. We knew about God and religion, but there was no faith statement in my immediate sphere.

Through those formative years of my childhood, I met with counsellors, family friends, and general acquaintances who had what I would now call a "noble intention," but unhelpful input.

This, of course, led me even deeper into what I think may be the most critical trap question in human history: "Why me!" Looking back, I asked this question many times, and I feel now that it is the question that fueled most of the issues I have had with God. In a relationship, we can't play the victim. When we do, it changes from a connection to a chore for the person constantly having to have strength for the other's emotional health.

"Why me?" and "what is wrong with me?" These were the fundamental questions of all my anger and shame. I was angry as a child. After all, I felt it was entirely my fault, and I felt shameful because I believed it. At age fourteen, it came out that my father had been cheating on my mother for an extended period with prostitutes.

Here is the kicker: to this day, I still do not know the truth surrounding the circumstances - there hasn't been much honesty surrounding what happened. As kids, we had it explained to us that Dad did a bad thing, and now we all had to suffer because of it. We would have to be naïve to think it was merely this simple. However, the deep sense of uncertainty surrounding the situation led me to blame myself for the breakdown of my family. After all, I was a challenging kid to handle. At least, that was what all the voices in my life had led me to believe.

As a boy, I had no idea that this was happening in my consciousness. But, as I explained earlier, we now know how spiritual and relational dynamics affect our responses to life situations. This relational breakdown between my parents was the basis for my acting out. I believe now that the breakdown happened long before the event, and perhaps this is what led me into some of the pains I hold now in my emotional realm.

Once my mother and Father had split, I had a great reason to begin the desperate spiral of need-based behaviour deeper than I had previously. I went from being a mildly angry child to a violent and manipulative teenager who had almost no administrative boundaries for behaviour socially. After all, the guidance of my moral structure had just proven to be corrupt. I lost all sense of what was right or wrong, and when it came to love, there was no way for me to understand its nature, let alone trust it. I became suspicious of any emotional connection, and those close to me knew about it.

What was taking place was deepening the perpetuation of my shame and anger towards the world, and I quickly, without even knowing Him, began to blame God. I remember many times when I suffered rejection or exposure that I cried out to God with a bargaining chip prayer: "God, if you would just do this one thing for me, I'll change, I promise." These prayers were founded on my preconceived idea of a God who was more like a dictator than a friend, and this all came with an unspoken question: "If you love me, prove it!"

When I hit the ripe old age of eighteen, I was in utter despair, climbing the wrong worldly ladders of women, drugs, drinking and crime. I soon found myself entangled in exporting pseudoephedrine out of the country. Inevitably, I had amounted to all I could muster to punish myself and the people I deemed responsible for my life. I was trying my hardest to survive while hating my existence, wanting to die while living in survival mode. It was a very perplexing situation. Thankfully, the need to survive won out.

I remember the night it all changed, and I met my Father. I had decided to walk from Heather and Steve's place to where we would all meet to take drugs. It was a cold night, and something was noticeably different. The feeling of the air being thin is so vivid to me still, years later, I would describe it as two realms colliding. God was so close to me at this moment. This was when it all changed, and God happened in my life. I received a phone call from one of the guys I was involved with that I had upset months before moving in with Steve and Heather.

I had since left the area and the friends that had helped me with the exportation of drugs. I had moved south back to where I grew up to get away from it all. I had done damage in too many relationships through lying, cheating, and accusing, and this guy was one of them. "We know where you are, and we are coming to get you," were the last words he spoke to me on the phone.

I remember the feeling of fear and helplessness that came from that conversation. It must have only been seconds, but it felt like hours went past as all the possible outcomes played through my mind. These people were dangerous, and I was scared. At this moment, I truly needed help. So I looked to the sky, mustered up all the courage I had to tell God what I thought of Him, and shouted,

"God, if you are real, you better prove yourself because I will kill myself. I am not letting these people take my life!"

It is ironic to think what I was trying to achieve was a way out of life. Yet, when the possibility presented itself, my survival instinct would kick in, and I would do the unexplainable to survive. It was a constant tension between hope and despair.

Looking back, perhaps this reaction was a little extreme. Although these people were scary and dangerous, my eighteen-year-old self was also quite dramatic. Regardless, God used the intense emotion of the situation to invade my world.

You are welcome to use your creativity for some of the fill-in words I used in that conversational piece with the Father. It was a raw, authentic, and honest exchange.

I was standing in a park all alone, filled with fear, anger, and pain, completely uncertain of my value to any living thing. Yet, I could still take you to the tree in Thalassa Park, South Australia, where this all took place. It was the most profound moment of my life. I had nothing left to give and nothing left to lose. I had strayed off the path to take a shortcut between the trees that filled the park. It was dark, and I was finally at the end of my rope.

I knew in my heart that this was it; I would take my life. Finally, everything they had said was right: I am in control, it is entirely my fault, and I can't do this anymore. It felt like an hour went past as all these thoughts came rushing in, but suddenly...

Before we continue with my account of that night, let me explain a few things that will bring context to the events that unfolded. Bear with me here as there is something He wants to unlock in you through this. One of the biblical precedents of this encounter is the 'suddenly' of God. So never neglect the 'suddenly' in scripture. Purely for reference, as to how willing God is to change a circumstance instantly, we need to look no further than the book of Acts.

Acts 2:2

*And suddenly, there came from heaven a sound like a mighty rushing wind, and it filled the entire house where they were sitting.*I choose to use this scripture here to try and attempt to describe what happened next.

It is essential to point out that my only exposure to God before this point was through an outreach bus in the area we had lived in called "The Buzz Bus." The name could have been better thought out considering those it was reaching: predominantly teenagers on drugs. In hindsight, it is pretty hilarious, although poorly named. On occasion, I had spoken with a man there named Steven Sherman, who had sparked my curiosity. At the time, I had no possible way of knowing how influential this man was to become in my life. He constantly challenged all my defence systems and was getting remarkably close to breaking through. I would have small victories in moving toward God, and then I would quickly lose interest, but Steve never stopped his pursuit. He sounds like someone else I know.

Almost instantly after I threatened God that night, I felt two hands thrust me into the ground. I began to weep uncontrollably. This was the beginning of my journey to intimate belonging. At that moment, I started to speak in a language I had never heard before and heard a voice both inside and outside of me. He explained that my value and worth to Him were not defined by my failures or anyone else's rejection of me, this message was in contradiction to my life so far. Instead, he desired to be with me and wanted to show me why.

After this all ended, I stood up and began to walk toward a friend's house. As I walked, He spoke again and asked me to turn around. As I did this, I could see myself there on my knees weeping, and this is what He said to me: "The choice is yours, follow me and live, or go back there and die." I was not faced with many options, but needless to say, as you are reading this book, I chose to follow Him.

For a few hours following this first encounter, I could not utter a single word in English. I remember running into a friend as I exited the park. It must have been evident that I had been weeping as he asked, "What happened to you?" I could not respond; I was completely and utterly overwhelmed by God's goodness to me at this moment.

In later weeks, as I journeyed through what happened to me with Steve, it was drawn to my attention that at this specific time, on that same night, he had gathered at the church to pray for me to meet with God specifically. This blew my mind for a few reasons: firstly, there was a group of people who would willingly spend their time praying with the purest desire to see a change in my life, and secondly, God listened to them on my behalf and showed up the way He did.

So often, people ask me, "Why do you think this happened to you?" It was not because God loved me more or because I was in desperate need, but because of the people connected to His heart that gathered in one place to ask Him to move. God's kind intentions toward me have changed my world forever through these humans.

It was not like I was scared, and I certainly did not have the language to describe what happened to me back then. The best way I can explain the feeling I experienced now is with the word 'reverence, which is commonly translated as 'fear' in scripture. It was as if the awe of who God is had struck me and left me in His wonder, and through this, I knew above all else that God was real and that His very being was loving-kindness.

If there is one piece of advice that I can give you that came from this moment, it is never to lose the wonder when it comes to God. As soon as we lose this, we lose sight of what could happen with God and begin to focus on what is happening around us. The wonder is the substance that will keep you in his presence.

So what was the prophetic purpose of this encounter? I will preface this because everything did not begin to "fall into place" from here on in, but there were a few powerful lessons I learned along the way that I will share with you throughout this book.

The first of these is this: the Father is a gentleman. Until this point, I had cried out to Him in desperation, blame, and of course, to bargain for what I wanted. I had never invited Him to show Himself or genuinely wanted to meet Him. I had viewed Him as distant and hidden due to my depravity, and as a result, our conversation, up until that point, was founded on the view of a God that was not close. I would describe God based on the picture painted of Him throughout the media and, unfortunately, in some cases, the expressions of the church.

It is a common misconception that God hides from us to provoke us to pursue him and seek him out. I won't dispute that there are seasons where He has withdrawn his presence for a purpose, but when it came to those who didn't believe in Him, He always was the one to initiate contact.

One of the primary reasons we miss this, if we are honest, is that we do not believe we are worth His time or the call He has placed on our lives. Perhaps more importantly, we don't think He sees us as worth loving. Don't worry; you are not alone in this. I want to refer you to some of the Bible greats; David spent most of his ministry perplexed about how God could love a mess like him.

At the last supper, the eleven disciples wondered if they were betrayers due to their lack of worth and value to God while John rested in His presence and heard His heartbeat. It is as if you can listen to the murmurings of the disciples as Jesus utters those words, "one of you will betray me." "Pssst, Matthew, did you tell Jesus those private doubts I shared with you?" "Am I the betrayer?"

Amazing the position we can find ourselves in when we stand outside of what God has said to be accurate, and through this, we begin to live in our negative view of ourselves. This is primarily due to our misunderstanding of the intent of God's heart toward us.

Papa wants to meet you, and He will stop at nothing. He will even bypass your expectation that has its foundation based on your view of Him to get to your heart. This was the beginning of His pursuit of my heart. He finally had my attention instead of having the extreme list of my needs to be met, and He was not going to let it fall by the wayside.

This encounter may wow you, and maybe you haven't had this kind of impacting experience. But imagine if your encounter was locked up in the questions you are asking. Then, instead of waiting for answers, you could be having a discussion, which will lead you toward a connectedness with God, that is the seedbed of transformation.

I want to challenge you to go into a place of intimacy with the Father and ask Him what it is you misbelieve about Him. If I had asked this question years ago, it would have been that I believed He was a dictator and not a friend, that He was far and not close, and that I had to behave a certain way to be loved. How I approached Him and thought about Him was hindering His ability to move in my life. Perhaps the concept of you being able to restrict God's movement is too much to swallow. I would encourage you to sit and ask Him about that, honestly. "Father, do I have the power to hinder your movement in my life?"

Let's dive into the next chapter together, but first, let me pray for you.

"Father, everything I have experienced and encountered, I pray, will be released in this life right now. I know you to be a God of intentional pursuit who still speaks and listens. I would ask that you walk around the potential hindrances and show my brother or sister the love you have shown me. Amen."

Adam Thurling

The Journey

THE STORY OF OUR FATHER'S PURSUIT CONTINUED IN INTIMACY.

Take a deep breath; the story that led to these theological thoughts was extensive and somewhat heavy. Let's lighten it up here and look at what I now believe based on these experiences. As with every great story, we need to snap out of our knowledge at some point and explore the truth and meaning behind it. Two words are used biblically to express what we call God's Word. Being the spoken Word, Rhema denotes a spiritual insight from an encounter with God and is also considered the direct utterances of Jesus. The second Word, Logos, points directly to the word as we know it is written in the Bible.

What I had experienced in this encounter was a Rhema word from God based on my value to him, and what I was about to learn over the next ten years was going to teach me how to believe what He spoke over me and back it up.

1 Peter 3:15

But in your hearts honour Christ the Lord as holy, always being prepared to make a defence to anyone who asks you for a reason for the hope that is in you; yet do it with gentleness and respect.

Again, I would like to stress - and will continue stressing - that what I share is the process of a continuing journey into the heart of God. I am not offering absolutes here but possibilities, which I hope you draw from and are invited to implement into your journey in knowing and becoming known by God.

I ended the last chapter with a statement about our ability to hinder God's movement in our lives. This is usually due to our belief systems regarding who He is, or rather, whom we think He is. There are many factors in play regarding our view of God. It can be determined by life experience, relational breakdown, church wounds, parental wounds or worse, and the list can go on. In your pursuit of truth, please drop your preconceived truths: they will only hinder your ability to be transformed. When we read scripture with preconceptions, we subconsciously read on a level that supports the 'truth' we already believe. We need to drop our preconceptions to be able to allow truth to define our experiences. Usually, if we don't do this, our expression will sound like we are moulding the Word around our experience, pain or reality.

We see this happen to Moses in the exodus account of his meeting with the burning bush. He experiences God and is given a mission that cannot fail because it is from the very mouth of God. Moses is then asked to lead.

In this scripture, Moses' view of himself gets in the way of his ability to accept what God is saying about him. Let's take a look.

Moses was running, even hiding at this point in his life. He needed some direction and God showed up and brought him his very own 'suddenly moment' to call him into greatness. Let's start with the initial encounter.

Exodus 3:2-4

And the angel of the Lord appeared to him in a flame of fire out of the midst of a bush. So he looked, and behold, the bush was burning; yet it was not consumed. And Moses said, "I will turn aside to see this great sight, why the bush is not burned.

When the Lord saw that he turned aside to see, God called to him out of the bush, "Moses, Moses!" And he said, "Here I am."

God calls Moses by name and out from his hiding and begins to speak destiny into Moses' life. This changes everything for him. It speaks of the Father's deep intimacy in knowing us before we are even aware of it. I remember the first moment in that park where the Father addressed me by name. I was deeply impacted by just being known by Him. Yet even in this seemingly obvious reality, if we allow its gravity to wash over us there is healing to lay hold of. Consider this: God deeply and intimately knows you. There is nothing you can do to change that.

What I love about Moses is that he heard the call and responded. It is always our choice to respond or disregard the call of God in our lives.

This freewill aspect of our nature is the truth, as evidenced by what we see Adam do in the garden. He heard the sound of the Lord coming and he chose to hide. The freewill mindset is what I hold on to as a reality in my relationship with God. We can hear the call and hear the cries of Jesus as He displays our value on the cross, but it is entirely our choice to engage with Him in these realities.

Further on in Exodus we see Moses (in a nutshell) tell God he can't do what He is asking because he does not feel qualified. For most of us this should sound incredibly familiar. However, the scripture says that God's anger was kindled toward Moses at this moment. I love that God's anger was kindled toward Moses' inability to place value on himself.

Moses had to see his value through the Jesus coloured lenses of our Father's eyes and not his own. As we read on in the scripture. If you can change how you view yourself, this will unlock your destiny as it did Moses'. When it comes to your view of yourself, God's plan is to meet you in your place of deficiency.

Exodus 4:13-14

But he said, "Oh, my Lord, please send someone else." Then the anger of the Lord was kindled against Moses, and he said, "Is there not Aaron, your brother, the Levite? I know that he can speak well. Behold, he is coming out to meet you, and when he sees you, he will be glad in his heart.

I have found this scripture intriguing for a long time. God's anger was kindled toward Moses not when he shirked his calling or failed, but instead when He didn't believe he was worthy of the calling.

Perhaps the deepest sin is in the moments we choose not to believe we are able, when God has called us so. In response to the cross, it is like saying that you are not worth love, based on your own opinion. I want to suggest to you that through Jesus' actions on the cross, we have lost the right to make that decision. This may be the only thing that would kindle God's anger towards us: that we wouldn't believe we are worth loving after being purchased at such a great price. This line of thinking may be the very thing that is hindering you from stepping into your destiny.

Have you ever lived a lifestyle of 'send someone else'? I know I have. Mainly on a subconscious, self- loathing level (which becomes reflective of my view of myself, not His view of me). To add to this, we see God's response to Moses steeped in mercy: "Is there not Aaron the Levite? I know he can speak well!" He answered the fear that Moses was carrying concerning his ability.

We need to remember it is okay to voice the fear in vulnerability with God without hopelessness attached. God showed Moses in this moment that He knew that Aaron had the ability. Yet what was more important was the calling was on Moses. This perhaps is the one of the earliest biblical pictures of the human condition that decides it is not worthy of what God has already destined it to be.

We find this mentality in the story of the prodigal son in the New Testament. The prodigal knows he can return home but does not believe he is worth the estate; he feels at this point that all he is worth is to become a servant in his Father's house. Sometimes we think we can come to God and only receive what we deserve.

I want to suggest that the Father does not deal in conversations surrounding your shortcomings. He sent Jesus to restore you to a high place, not a place of groveling, and through Jesus what you deserve has been redefined on your behalf. You are worth dying for.

Luke 15:19

I am no longer worthy of being called your son. Instead, treat me as one of your hired servants.

When the Father is faced with our self-loathing thoughts such as, "I am not worthy," He meets us with a ring and a robe. How we decide to walk in that inheritance is up to us. We can wear it boldly as a restored son, or we can wear it like we are not worthy and miss the blessing, or worse, neglect the inheritance. When we spend so much of our time in His presence saying sorry to feel relief from our perceived guilt (based on what we think He requires), we miss out on what He is doing in us and through us. When we engage with God, we need to do it from our restored position of being a son, not from a place of being a servant.

Luke 15:21-22

And the son said to him, 'Father, I have sinned against heaven and before you. I am no longer worthy of being called your son.' But the Father said to his servants, 'Bring the best robe quickly, put it on him, put a ring on his hand, and shoes on his feet.

The Father, (almost offensively to us), ignores his son's words of self-loathing and unworthiness, disregarding His act of 'repentance' as we see it.

Instead, he proceeds to celebrate his return instantly. He does not even respond to His son's guilt and shame mentality. Could we think about this for a second? That truth will release you from years of religious abuse of self and send you on a crash course of self-acceptance. We seek vulnerability with God while trying to deny vulnerability in our lives and wonder why we are so confused. It is okay to be a mess. Many of us have chosen to take our inheritance over our relationship at some stage in our lives. For me, this statement has taken many forms.

My version of taking my inheritance over connection is that I wanted to have it all right now without the hard work that a relationship required with God. When I say hard work, I do not mean simply reading my Bible, praying and making sure I didn't swear. I am alluding to undoing my view of Him based on my expectations that have their foundation firmly wrapped up in assumptions regarding His character.

As humans, we struggle with justice, and when it comes to our version of justice, we will often land in the place of condemnation for others and ourselves without much hesitation. When we weigh up God's justice against our own, the reality is that His version looks like mercy to the guilty, while ours primarily results in exposure and condemnation. Thankfully we are living in His reality and not ours. It is a ludicrous position to take the condemnation route when we have a God-like Jesus, and can I suggest that self-loathing is the one thing that angers Him more than anything. It kindles a fire in Him because of the price he has paid for you to be with Him regardless of your mistakes.

The Journey

It will serve you well to note the Father's subsequent actions in the famous parable of the prodigal. The son tries to strike a deal to become a servant. Think about it for a second. Does the Father even raise his voice? No. His following actions are of restoration. The Father knows there will be a journey regarding his son's repair through his view of himself. Perhaps he understands that the journey the son is about to go on is one of believing he is worth loving at all after what he has done.

This, in my opinion, is where grace meets humanity. It is not in the place of unworthiness but in the reality that God knows how hard we are on ourselves and waits for us to understand our value to Him. The simple act of his son returning home gives him enough to work with. He desires to begin to re-establish His position and better yet, restore His Son's inheritance. This is scandalous grace, and you can almost feel as you read through these scriptures the Jewish audience rising in anger against the God they serve. This is a love that is unbridled and steeped in freedom.

It may be offensive to you for me to say, but the Father skips over your repentance in celebration of your return. This reality will change your approach to Him. We spend so much energy - perhaps at no fault of our own - trying to feel God's approval for us by living to a standard that allows us to believe we are acceptable. The paradox here is that He died because we could not live according to the standard required by law. What if His approval was the foundation and motivation that we live from? Instead of being motivated to righteousness, we would be motivated into connection, which, in turn, would inspire a righteous lifestyle.

The Greek word for righteousness most commonly found in the Bible is *diksiosyn*. In this context, we can find it around eighty times in the New Testament, making it the most predominant definition of the word. It means "righteousness" in "meeting the requirements of God's law." So, to be righteous is to live in the fulfilment of the law, which in turn is what Jesus achieved for us on the cross. But what law are we to fulfil now to become the righteousness of Christ? This is an important question to ask, as we know that the law in the context of the Old Testament was not done away with but added to when Christ fulfilled it! So knowing that the old law is not finished but added to, what law do we need to fulfil to be deemed right before God?

The answer is found in the person of Jesus, and he makes it plain. Throughout the New Testament, Jesus establishes a new law, and that law is the one of love.

To be righteous, we must be able to live as Love in and through Christ. Regarding living as love, it must also be said that to love is the very fulfillment of the old law. God has defined himself as love, and Jesus was the sacrifice of love. That is, of course, if you believe that Jesus was the fulfilment to, and not the full stop on, the Old Testament law. Through love, we are known by God and know God.

This divine knowing and being known is the bedrock of our transformation, not the "become righteous to be acceptable" model we have all been taught. Instead, you have been called righteous and now are invited into a conversation surrounding our relational response to God. Some feel this is risky because it can sound like empowerment to sin, while others realise that to be in a relationship in its truest sense is a far deeper requirement to our salvation than simply following the rules. We have been taught outside of a relational context that we must live up to the standards implied to be loveable. I want to suggest that when you fall in Love with God, the focus turns from the rules and your eyes become fixed on the relationship. You might be able to say that if we live by the rules, there is a definable line in which we can feel safe to be accepted without having to do much work in being known to God. But this concept takes any responsibility out of our hands and leaves us where it is all God's responsibility. In a relationship, there is work to be done in honour of one another to keep the connection. This is why I believe God made us the way we are: in need of connection to survive.

The relational model places you in the embrace of God's Love, but it also asks you to love it back in return. It's not about forgetting how to be "a good Christian"; it is about falling in love that provokes this desire to please God. That is why the law is fulfiled by love and nothing else.

It is as if the Father is wooing us into His presence through a gentle reminder of our value to Him. Naturally, as we fall in Love with Him, our desires fall into place and align with His. I understand this is risky because it goes against our reality that some people will abuse such love, and we should challenge this. The unfortunate reality is that the scripture clarifies that there will be those who refuse to partake in this kind of love. I can't control it, and I can't change it, but what I can do is Love like Christ and hope that it transforms their hearts.

This is a process of 'growing in love'. I don't know of any marriage being perfect from the instant the register is signed. It is a process of working at love while living in a reality of contractual completion. This is the gospel; we are a perfect completion in spirit while on a journey to believing this in our flesh, both complete and on a journey.

We have been given grace and mercy established within this journey of process.

What if we changed our mindset to 'I belong; therefore, I will believe' instead of believing to belong? To add to this, I will end this long-winded explanation with the words of Jesus, who is about the fulfillment of the law. A Pharisee approached him in Mark chapter 12 and asked, "Which is the greatest of the laws?" His response: "The most important is, Hear, O Israel: The Lord our God, the Lord is one. And you shall love the Lord your God with all your heart and with all your soul and with all your mind and with all your strength.' The second is this: You shall love your neighbour as yourself.' There is no other commandment greater than these."

This looks like a response based Christianity instead of a reaction based one. I respond to His Love; therefore, because of love, I become - instead of, He has died, and I need to react by living in a way that is acceptable to Him to be accepted. My flesh struggles with this because I desire, in most instances, to step into the place of the Holy Spirit when it comes to someone's transformation. I have only now begun to trust the same Holy Spirit in me to work in someone else.

After my initial encounter with the Father, I searched desperately for another meeting with the God I had met in the park. At the time, I had the absolute pleasure of being looked after (as I have mentioned) by Steven Sherman who knew how to love like the Father. Unfortunately, the journey I had to go on was messy and soon after this encounter I started to perpetuate the same realities that I was living out before all of this had happened . I quickly forgot how relentless His pursuit of me was in love and started to live out my need to prove I was acceptable.

This is how we disqualify ourselves while God sits patiently waiting for us to return to the truth. We don't need to "do" something to be loved in our initial encounter.

I did all the right things; I battled my desires, read my Bible, went to Bible study, tried to stop swearing, and even led people to Jesus. That first year was a wonder-filled one! We led twenty-seven drug addicts to Christ and I got to baptise seven of them myself. But as time went by, something was missing. I knew that God loved me because he had told me so, but I didn't believe it for some reason unknown to me at the time. Or perhaps worse, I had begun to forget it.

The lesson of the difference between knowing and believing is where the heart journey begins. The longest eighteen-inch journey you will go on is the one from your head to your heart. I was spending far more time dealing with my "sin" than with God. Nevertheless, He had intentions of intimacy and I had to come to a place where I was willing to stop looking at my faults and start listening to His voice. This was the beginning of intimacy between us.

Intimacy. We hear this word a lot in our church culture these days, and for a good reason. We are currently in a reformation of the church that is healing hearts and mending church wounds. God is reconciling us to Himself through revelation and understanding of His nature, and the good news is that the church is mostly buying into it and growing through it.

For me, all my conceivable realities lie in my intimacy with God. When I am distant, I am driven by my fear of exposure and the desire to please Him in order to be accepted. When I am close, I am sustained by the personal revelations of my Papa, knowing that He has never desired me based on my behaviour.

Let's dive into a biblical example to support what I am talking about. But before we do, prepare your heart. The knowledge in your head may be challenged here or it could be simply affirmed. This could be the beginning of change for you, or I might solidify your suspicions. Either way, I implore you to posture your heart in a way that says, 'I am open, Lord'.

John is our best example in this arena of intimacy; he rested on the heartbeat of Jesus while the disciples wondered if they were the betrayer. John rested in intimacy, which left him in a place of revelation. He understood who he was at that moment, while his friends forgot who they were within themselves and the value they carried through the eyes of Jesus.

Let's look at these scriptures and see what we can draw out of them for our lives.

John 13:21-22

After saying these things, Jesus was troubled in his spirit and testified, "Truly, truly, I say to you, one of you will betray me." The disciples looked at one another, uncertain of whom he spoke.

This has always baffled me; they looked around at each other uncertain whom He was talking about. Wait, what?

Let's picture this for a second. You have eleven disciples sitting around a table, motioning to each other about themselves. I imagine it would have sounded something like this: "Hey Matthew, did you at all, maybe, mention to Jesus the doubts I shared with you in private? I mean... I didn't mean what I said. So is it me that Jesus thinks is the betrayer?"

Their uncertainty in this exposes something in them that I can relate to. Insecurity and self-doubt that inevitably stems from a doubt of their genuine love for God and their ability to accept who they were in God. More importantly, their ability to believe that the God right before their eyes loved them. Too often, we have sat in the position of the eleven and wondered in insecurity despite our first love experience. It leads us to live out our faith vicariously through those we deem to be of more value to God. We need to become like the one who trusted his position in Christ and positioned himself in intimacy.

John 13:23-25

One of his disciples, whom Jesus loved, was reclining at the table at Jesus' side, so Simon Peter motioned to him to ask Jesus of whom he was speaking. So that disciple, leaning back against Jesus, said, "Lord, who is it?"

There was an exposure of heart for the disciples at the table at this moment. A divine lesson had taken place for them, and if we're not careful, we'll miss what John was encountering and what Jesus was encouraging for us all.

John was tightly tucked in an embrace with Jesus; he was close and listening to the heart of God. I am sure he senses the pain in Jesus' initial words.

This is where we see the exposure of their hearts take place. John's posture was triggering a large amount of insecurity at the table. The disciples, who were just feet away from Jesus, could not even muster up the courage to ask Jesus the question that they were freaking out about. This is what happens next in this passage.

One disciple motions to John to say, "You are

close to Him; he trusts you!" This tenderises my heart and as I type this, I wish you could feel the emotion it stirs up in me to be close to our God.

This is a confirmation of disconnection in the relationship. It was not that Jesus was not accessible; it was the mindset that "Jesus loves John more" that had denied them access. To you, this mindset may sound more like this: "Why wasn't I invited to hang out with the pastor?"

These are beliefs we build in our lives based on lies we have learned about our intimacy with God and people. First, we fear stepping into a relationship because of the potential impending rejection, and then we blame others and God for our lack of self-worth. This cycle robs us of freedom in His presence and instead of going to the source, we ask someone else for access.

John 13:24

So Simon Peter motioned to him to ask Jesus of whom he was speaking.

At this moment, John, right on cue, delves deeper into intimacy with Jesus. He steps in and asks the question from that place of intimacy. "Lord, who is it?" I can understand why people outside of intimacy would find it hard to delve into an area they don't feel invited into. We may not have to ask who will betray Him, but we have more profound questions about our identity that require extreme trust. John was sure he was not the betrayer and, in my opinion, was so caught up in an embrace that the thought didn't even cross his mind.

Perhaps if we delve deeper into what Simon Peter could have been feeling in this moment, we would find a common denominator that we have not been willing to face. Maybe the real question being asked of John is one of access.

It is not John's place, responsibility, or problem that others are not positioned in intimacy. Still, religion has taught us we need to push people to where we determine they need to be. I want to suggest that if we model a "John" lifestyle, people will see the depth of knowing God and being known to God in our lives and, in turn, step in with us.

The direct result of John's intimacy was the revelation of whom Jesus spoke. While the disciples were busy searching their hearts to lower their anxiety levels, John was steadfast in knowing the Love Jesus had for him.

John 13:26

Jesus answered, "It is he to whom I will give this morsel of bread when I have dipped it." So when he had dipped the morsel, he gave it to Judas, the son of Simon Iscariot.

Where do you stand today? Are you in a state of fear-driven performance Christianity? Or, like John, are you resting on the heartbeat of God that intentionally has a rhythm that quickens love in you?

We know that Jesus had hope for Judas because of the very definition of love, as found in 1 Corinthians 13; Love bears all things, hopes all things, and endures all things. If only Judas had allowed himself to meet with love, things might have been different that night. But regardless, our Saviour was always going to the cross in love.

The primary difference between living a Judas or a John lifestyle is this; John rested in intimacy while Judas made decisions from deficiency.

In a way, I can understand how Judas felt. Maybe he was the first victim of what we now know as 'tall poppy syndrome.' However, I am also led to wonder what the other disciples were thinking as they watched John get something they were missing. I am confident, as well as you are, that we have all had these moments with God, the "why them" moments, quickly followed by the "where are my blessings?"

Don't live in the regret of deficiency when intimacy is on offer. We see Judas' experience in repentance as similar to the spiritual abuse we put ourselves through to gain back God's acceptance. Remember, your justice is far harsher on you than God's is.

Your blessings and relationship with the Father are locked up in your gaze at the circumstance. Once you fall in love with Jesus, instead of seeing the prize, you will no longer desire to compete but enjoy the party that love has invited you into.

Don't be like the vast majority, whispering to others to ask what God is thinking and saying about you. Be bold. Rest on His heart.

Expect the 'suddenly' of God in your life. Set it as a daily expectation and be bold enough as a son to remind God that, well, quite frankly, it is your right as a son to have access to the king's presence.

Never allow your view of yourself to define how He sees you. Always enable the truth to dictate that, and the truth is that you are a son.

Make loving God the principal thing. After all, we are people who love to self-focus. As a result, we navel-gaze our sin instead of looking at the Redeemer, who is the source in which we find the ability to live free from our stuff!

Walk wholeheartedly in your inheritance, know your place in the Kingdom and better still, accept it. Sit with the Father in this for a while. There is a large amount to process after this. So don't move on too fast.

Go and grab your journal. I challenge you to think about a few moments where you have lived out this cycle of coveting others' depth with God. Ask yourself, "How did I feel, think, and act when they were blessed or when they were invited to a leader's house?" Be honest about it and invite the Father into these deficiencies.

Father, today I pray that you would take hold of this child's heart. Would you help them begin the long road from the head to the heart? So that they will genuinely desire to know you.

Adam Thurling

The Journey

THE STORY IN THE LIE OF UNWORTHINESS

As I touched on earlier regarding the prodigal, my journey (much like that of the character in the parable Jesus teaches from), was primarily learning how to wear the inheritance as a son. I had no idea of the depth of pain I had lived through. I almost walked past it as if it was an achievement of survival and it certainly provided for me an identity in the church. I was someone who had a story to tell and people seemed to love that. The culture of the church I ended up in after the years I had spent with Steve had the potential to feed the ego that lay in my story.

Within this section, I want to delve a little deeper into the lie of unworthiness and tackle it head-on, helping you see it for what it is. There will be no dancing around the topic here. I desire to respect your personhood and empower you to ask some hard questions about the cultures you have attached yourself to. I want to empower you to make healthy decisions surrounding your faith and journey. To give you voice to your concerns, while offering wisdom to separate them from the pain of our judgments. You will not find me empowering your pain. Instead, you will be given the keys to help you love through the pain and trials. This is so you can find freedom from judgment. God does not perpetuate the pain in our lives. However, He takes pleasure in transforming what was intended for evil and turning it into something good.

Disclaimer alert: before I talk about this I will touch on cultures that are, in my opinion, not helpful to the healing journey or how we view the Father. I firmly believe that culture only gets its power in how you allow it to define you. Primarily, you alone are responsible for you. It is not the culture that is the problem, it is your lack of self-love that causes you to get hurt by its influence. This is often founded on an apparent inability to receive love.

We need to quit blaming the leaders and the churches. Instead, let's start taking responsibility for our destination. Now, this is not to say that if you are in a situation where you are being controlled or spiritually abused, that it is okay. You do need to love through it, but self-love will empower you to find your value and change the circumstance you are in. Loving yourself will provoke a few things that will free you to love through many things without judgment and help you see where your faults lie. It always takes two to tango!

I will mention some pain and frustration I experienced, but it is essential to know (in defence of the parties involved) that my reaction perpetuated the pain I experienced. It was not purely the fault of the churches, or the leadership involved. When it comes to relational breakdown or strife, I hold the position that we are all responsible for mending the breakdown, whether we are wrong or right, as the ambassadors of Christ. Ultimately, (again, I will emphasise) we are not responsible for the people who have hurt us, but we are accountable for our response. So I want to encourage you to only ever respond and never react.

Oh, how I wish I had that wisdom a few years ago. Even now, this is the battle of my life.

One of the main things about inheritance is that you will never live in the benefits of it unless you genuinely believe you are worth it. In a worldly context, we could place a relational paradigm here. You will only walk in the benefits of the relationship with your leaders, pastors and friends if you genuinely believe you are worth loving. I wish I could express to you the countless times I have had leaders invite me into relationships where, sadly, the thing that damaged these relationships (for me) was the reality that I didn't believe I was worth loving. I could not trust their intention because I had defined the experience before it happened. This was founded on my previous experiences and bitterroot expectations that love was a loaded gun in life and could do damage at any moment. How wrong I was. Let me take a second to define what I mean by bitteroot expectation.

Hebrews 12:15

See to it that no one fails to obtain the grace of God; that no "root of bitterness" springs up and causes trouble, and by it, many become defiled;

A bitteroot expectation is where we have had an experience that will define the future outcome of things that display similar opportunities or feelings of attachment. For example, my childhood experience of love was very manipulative and somewhat destructive, so I would expect that this would be the future outcome when I felt any kind of love. As the feeling became more substantial, I would start to self-sabotage and push whoever was getting too close away from me as a form of protection. If we all spend some time pondering on this, we will find patterns of expectation that have defiled many opportunities and relationships based on a momentary experience we had years ago. It may sound like this: "All churches are the same!" "Love isn't worth it."

Honestly, this is a powerful revelation, and you should spend some time pondering on and breaking off any bitter roots that may have come through painful experiences. I must give recognition where it is due as I learnt this reality in my life through the School of Prophets. It is a profoundly transforming understanding and I encourage you to look into it.

In these moments, I became gripped by insecurity and would furiously look for the moment where they let me down so I could shut them out. Predetermining the relationship and controlling its outcome is where I thought I found safety, but I was destroying everything I craved.

For you, the manifestation of this may sound something more like this:

"Why won't they invite me?"

"Why did such and such make the cut?"

"Why them and not me?"

Or even worse: "I have been setting up and packing down these chairs for them for a year now, and still I am not invited in."

These statements should be red flags for us all. Lying dormant underneath the surface of this pain is a belief that we are not valued by someone; when in actual fact, our expectations have set them up to fail.

Here we start a blame cycle and begin to shift the responsibility onto them for how we feel.

I will sound like a broken record here, but this is the most transformational reality; we are only responsible for how we respond and not how we perceive we have been treated. Can you imagine Jesus calling time out; "Guys, this is unfair how you are treating me and I am starting to wonder whether you are all worth it."

Essentially, this is what we do when we allow a breakdown to occur based on our perceived expectations of our leaders. Like them, we forget that Jesus was human, so we neglect grace because we want justice.

I am aware that this could profoundly affect you, as we have all walked this out in some form or another. However, I want to provide you with some keys to move past this, which I have learned through my journey. Honestly, I have faced some tough things regarding spiritual and emotional abuse in the church and have at times felt justified in shutting people out. Unfortunately for us all, we can't find any biblical backing to support that behaviour. As frustrating as this is, there is great freedom in loving through the trial of a relationship.

Matthew 5:24

Leave your gift there before the altar and go. First, be reconciled to your brother, and then come and offer your gift.

So, how do we achieve this? Let me tell you another story.

After my initial encounter, you would be forgiven for thinking that I was instantly a fantastic Christian and was completely healed from all the mess in my life and walking free.

This was very far from the truth.

One thing we need to be careful with when it comes to an encounter and radical change, is something I would like to call "transferable idols." In the world of drugs, women, and alcohol, one of my significant idols was power. This led me into relationships where I would manipulate and control as a Christian to feel I still had authority, and I found this need met in leadership. It was time to ask myself some hard questions while facing this. It was never intentional, but due to my experiences, I had learnt a normal behaviour that could play no part in the Kingdom, and my perceived reality was about to collide with the truth of my situation. This is the fabric of grace, that the Father was unwilling to leave me in a place of pain and was intentional about finding my freedom.

Leadership and the influence it gave me provided an easy way to fill an unhealthy desire in my life.

I had successfully transferred and continued to feed what I was serving in the world (the need for power through fear and importance) into the church by becoming a leader. Six years after my encounter, I moved on from Steve's church and spent a few months wandering. Eventually, I planted in a church in Adelaide's south called Miracle City Church. The leaders were charismatic and their faith was attractive. After attending for a few years, I found myself on the team and helping to facilitate a young adult's ministry which, in my eyes was growing well. Unfortunately for the church and myself, I was unaware of or couldn't see my unhealthy needs being met. I was getting these needs met by my church, which was very messy. Let me flesh out what I mean by transferable idols. These are the things that we do while living away from God, like using intimidation to gain power, money, popularity etc.

It's when we transfer a need in our life that we feel we have been delivered from and find the same satisfaction in something else. This could be deemed a great thing from the outside when it is rooted in the same need that Papa was delivering us from in the first instance.

The best example of this is insecurity.

This is somewhere I feel the church has maybe made some bad decisions. We see people desperate to serve and we don't take the time to ask why? Service is almost always a great thing; however, when we transfer our idol of insecurity and neediness into the church and remedy it by serving to be seen, are we helping the church or God? Or are we merely finding a way to avoid dealing with the real issue?

This will work for a while until you feel unseen and then start talking trash about your leaders because they don't seem to be valuing what you do for them. Can I suggest this is not service but instead self-serving?

My plea to you is to search your heart when stepping into any form of ministry or service to see whether you need it. If you do, there is a good chance that you are transferring an idol from somewhere else in your life.

Through this understanding, it is also important to realise that these realities do not disqualify you; you merely need to be aware of them, and they will lose their power. However, if you do not pay attention to these things, I can assure you that they will surface.

When they do, you will feel justified in your anger or frustration while you are actually falling into a trap you can't see.

As I was saying earlier in this chapter, one thing I did was transfer my need for power into leadership positions.

Let's get back to me.

Why did I do this? Was it a conscious decision to be a person who would use people to get what I wanted? Of course not. I was not even aware that I was hurting people, and worse, that I was using them. As I grew into the faith, I was leaving the same kind of painful trail in my wake as I had in my life before my awakening to Christ. I had an excuse now: God was in control, and He wanted things this way.

The fact is, I was hurting people by pushing them away and not letting them get too close. So what I thought was just a natural progression of the relationship was a self-sabotaging, self-fulfilling prophecy. The problem here was that instead of dealing with the issues in my life with God (through relationship). I kept them at a distance by serving.

The unspoken prophetic word I was speaking over my life was this: "I will never make it, I will never be seen, and I will never be truly valued." In my eyes no leader, pastor, or mentor could see my calling and anointing. This was the perceived reality, but it was not the truth. I now know that I was seen, valued and even given opportunities in abundance. The real problem was likely that they had to spend more time managing my need to feel loved, rather than seeing any fruit from their investment. It is taxing for any leader to have to stand in the place that God should be standing in our lives; to fulfil the void God should be fulfilling.

If we keep running to our leaders, He will simply wait in grace for our focus to shift onto Him and in this, we will meet our dear friend called breakdown.

I had met love, but I had not let love meet my needs. I was very capable of filling those needs in my life and God became an avenue in which I could gain my identity. But instead of having it in Him, I got it through Him. The reality was that I didn't trust the Father with my destiny. I was so busy working toward being someone that others looked at as vital that I forgot how to be loved!

Why do we do this?

This cycle is firmly wrapped up in who we think the Father is based on our perceptions. We have been taught a narrative based on our negative view of God's intention in the creation story for all of our lives. There is a truth in this story that will set us free if we can drop our perceptions. I realised that most, (if not all) of my issues with God were based on the foundations of what I believed in Him. A good friend said this to me one day,

> *"This is what we believe about God: He created man and destined for us to fail, then punished us for that failure which looked like separation, so that He could kill His own Son in order to be reunited with us."*
>
> *"And we wonder why we struggle to trust Him."*
>
> *- David Tensen –*

Before this conversation with David in Narre Warren, I had encounter upon encounter with the Father. I eventually understood why and what Papa was trying to communicate with me through this conversation with David.

So, let's explore this. For me, most of my "sinful" behaviours were wrapped up in my God view. The cycle would always begin with me determining that I was not worthy of God's presence. That then quickly led to repentance, which looked more like self-loathing than it did embracing forgiveness. I believed God was angry at my inability to live in a pure and holy manner, but this was actually the mindset that God was trying to challenge. Once I had dispelled a few myths that I had believed about Him, my life was radically changed forever. Perhaps the best part of this newfound reality was the change I felt toward Him, impacting how I interacted with Him. It completely changed how I approached service to Him and engaged with Him.

Are you ready for another story?

So, many years passed by in my faith journey. I had managed to get myself some recognition in the local church I was a part of in the southern suburbs of Adelaide. This is where I had begun the downward spiral of finding my identity in a leadership position again. In my eyes, they did not see the asset I was to them, which triggered some very familiar pains in my life. The young adult group I was helping to lead was growing, and my influence was a large part of that. However, my need was not being met. When our needs are unmet, we begin to form blind spots in our emotional realm, especially when we highly value people's opinions.

My crash began after a long struggle of fighting with pastors and suspecting the worst about relationships. I went from being the pleasant guy most people liked (and some even loved) to someone driven by bitterness and suspicion.

This is where my intentional and loving God intervened.

But 'suddenly.'

The community I was a part of for this season was an unwilling partner in God's plan to bring me to my knees. As I share this, I would like to honour certain parties who may not otherwise know that I look at them as people whom God used to form me, mature me, and wake me up to some hard truths in my life.

Pastor David Hall and His Father Tim are two people who got the bitter end of a long process of me dying (in a spiritual sense), and they deserve the honour. I have always believed that people like these, as well as guys, like Steve Sherman, get to partner in all my victories because of the part they have played. So here I honour you all for your role in this journey.

Back to the story.

It was in this place of pain that the journey to freedom began. I remember one Sunday morning sending my pastor an email explaining why I was leaving his church and all the things I felt he had done wrong in this process. It was my final attempt to find some relief from my shame. None of this was my fault, but lying dormant in my subconscious was the hope that someone could free me from my guilt by taking the blame.

In my subconscious, I knew that I was perpetuating spiritual abuse on myself. Still, shame's grip made me hide from this reality and focus solely on the guilt that I felt others were giving me through broken relationships. Obviously, this couldn't have been my fault entirely. Oh, how wrong I was.

In every relational breakdown, there are two people responsible, but we need to focus our attention on our end of the issue and not theirs. The truth is that we have the power to not only free ourselves from the brokenness that comes with relational breakdown but we also have a role through our response that can help or hinder the other party involved. This is where we need to learn how to take responsibility for the relationship instead of focusing on the behaviours that caused the issue.

When we do this, we take very seriously the idea of laying it all at the altar and being reconciled with our brother. I will clarify "taking responsibility" later. Still, before we continue the story, I want to empower you to see that you indeed have the power in every relationship, to walk in restoration instead of breakdown. Whether you are justified or guilty in the relationship it is entirely on you to step into restoration. This looks like actively seeking out the heart of others instead of shutting them out. It's time to invite people in.

Years before this point in my life, a friend and brother of mine, Nathan Wilby and his fantastic wife Shanti had moved up to a community in Byron Bay to do a ministry school. He had come down to visit for a night while I was still in Adelaide, and little did I know that this would change my life.

The night I caught up with Nathan in 2012, something awoke in me that began to spark a fresh hope. By this point I had damaged my reputation via a series of poor relational decisions that had resulted in public outbursts and I was feeling completely and utterly alone. I remember this night because I had come to the end of a repeated cycle that would have landed me back in the same church living out the same self-sabotaging abuse that God was trying to stop in my life. Without this time with Nathan, I firmly believe that I would have gone running back to the things that had been feeding my self-worth my whole life, if that had been the case I would have never have ended up in a heap on the floor in my saviour's embrace.

Speaking with him that night, I felt somehow both seen and exposed as he challenged where I was. He could see the pain but did not empower it, instead He asked me to come on a journey. He called me up and not out. It wasn't about my behaviour, it was about the answer. If you asked Nathan today, I am confident he would say he had no idea what I needed, but he knew I needed something.

Nathan made me feel that I belonged with him on this journey. He didn't present it to me as though I needed help but instead as an invitation to come on a journey of discovery. Nathan offered me no more shame and placed no blame. In this conversation, I experienced the simple reality that it is okay to be a mess, but God does not want us to stay there.

This sounds suspiciously like the actions of Jesus with the disciples. We see this in Jesus' approach to the fisherman and the workers of His day. He was whispering something far more profound than "come with me." If you had become a fisherman, you had also become a failure in the Jewish system. you hadn't made the grade to become something influential, like a Rabbi. So, we see Jesus model something unique in choosing who He chose to follow Him. Have you ever explored the moment Jesus invited the fisherman to follow Him? There are some significant realities that can help us in our journey.

These realities challenge a culture of performance that tells us, based on our appearance or circumstance, whether we are called or not. Instead, Jesus utters three simple words that restore us all in the midst of what we consider our failure: "Come follow me."

Matthew 4:18-22

While walking by the Sea of Galilee, he saw two brothers, Simon (who is called Peter) and Andrew his brother, casting a net into the sea, for they were fishermen. And he said to them, "Follow me, and I will make you fishers of men." So immediately they left their nets and followed him. And going on from there, he saw two other brothers, James, the son of Zebedee and John, his brother, in the boat with Zebedee their father, mending their nets, and he called them. Immediately they left the boat and their father and followed him.

We see them drop their nets and follow Jesus without any hesitation. This seems rather radical, doesn't it? However, what was happening was that Jesus was restoring their standing in a public way, calling to them and essentially saying, "You are worth it! Come follow me."

Galilee was known to have one of the strictest sects of Judaism around, and there was a great sense of pride that came with becoming an influential member of the rabbinic system. The Father in this story would have carried great hope that one of His sons would be chosen by a rabbi to be taught, because it would have brought significant influence and standing in their lives.

Why didn't the Father argue with his sons when they stopped working and followed this guy? He was probably too busy crying due to what this meant for his family. This was a very public moment of restoration amid what the system had deemed to be failures, and along came Jesus to restore their position in the community and their view of themselves. The invitation by Jesus did not come with preconceived ideas. At this point they didn't know, think or feel He was any more important than the next rabbi. They were invited into belonging before they believed. We need to start taking this position: we don't need to believe to belong. Instead, we belong and with this, we hear Jesus inviting us to believe.

It is a gift we all have to be able to make someone feel seen and heard, a gift to offer redemption in a journey filled with relational value. It is healing at its finest. When you feel this, you come alive.

Once again I had found myself in a broken state where I thought I was failing. But my problem was in my ability to see my value. That's what kept me there. I thank God for Nathan that night. If I hadn't felt seen and challenged I don't know where I would be standing today.

When Nathan left, I had decided to take a risk by moving to Byron, but it didn't end there. In the coming weeks, I experienced God's presence in ways I had never dreamt of.

This sparked some of the most profound revelations I hold onto today in who the Father is. In the next chapter, I will explore the enticing model that I now believe Jesus has invited us to partner with.

Can you hear the call? "Come follow me. Let me show you what you are worth so we can do something great together!"

Who in your life can you extend the olive branch of freedom in belonging to?

Father, I pray that the extent of this revelation would be fully known to our hearts. Would you tear down the yoke of religious expectation in our lives and free us from ourselves. We love you, Father and adore all you are doing and have done.

The Journey

THE STORY OF THE FATHER'S NATURE

When I tell the story of unworthiness and mention that it sparked for me some of the most profound revelations from which I live today, I have to revert to where it all began. In late 2012, I was in a pretty painful situation. As I mentioned in the last chapter, Nathan had come down and helped me see my value in this time, but what made me pack up my bags and move so quickly? It was about a three-week turnaround until I had found myself sleeping on the floor of an open shed in the foothills of Byron Bay. Was this a purely emotive decision based on a desperate need to feel that I could escape?

Let me say this: if we make our decisions purely from an emotional place, we will provoke a seriously flawed mentality in which we base the voice of God on our needs instead of His presence.

An encounter with God backed my decision to move away from my safety net and inevitably kill the cycle of shame in my life. However, it never is that easy.

A few days after Nathan's visit, I found myself in a strange encounter. I remember one night I was having the most bizarre encounter with an angelic presence that led me into a dream.. At this time of my life I lived with some guys from my local church in North Plympton South Australia. As I explained in the last chapter, I was in a heap of pain and something needed to break. On this night I was lying in my room at the end of myself in a depressed state and I wanted almost nothing to do with God or His people.

I was burnt out. I lay in hopelessness and felt complete uncertainty about who I was and who God was. All of a sudden while laying in my room, I heard worship music sung at the top of someone's lungs. In my frustrated state I stormed out of my room and yelled at my housemate. "Would you just stop singing? It is so annoying". He looked at me bewildered and said he wasn't singing at all. I went back into my room with a feeling of total confusion. This continued, I heard worship playing again and it was not just singing but full-on worship music. As this was happening I was so frustrated that I started yelling, "Just turn it down, please."

He instantly replied, "I am not playing music." I was so confused and angry that I had no idea what to think at this stage. I wanted to escape anything that looked like or sounded like God. Then it happened as I lay in my room, I heard a loud "thud" on the window and the sound of someone praying in tongues.

Instantly, I fell back into my bed, gold dust covered me from head to toe, and I found myself praying uncontrollably. This was an encounter with an angelic force for preparation for what was to come. Now that I had a taste of the glory God had to offer I was hungry for more. This encounter lasted for thirty to forty minutes and once it was over I felt a sense of envelopment.

He was with me, even in my most broken place. This sparked a revival in my spirit and a last-ditch effort to press into Him and His plan amid all this chaos.

A few days later while worshiping with a friend, Rocky, and a girl named Elly, who is now his wife, these strange encounters continued. Rocky stopped me mid worship with a look of awe and confusion on his face. He explained that he could see an angel spanning its wings behind me. Almost as soon as he stopped speaking I could no longer play the guitar as pools of oil began dripping from my hands. This oil was so thick that it was preventing me from gripping the guitar. I hold onto these few days dearly as a reminder of God's pursuit of my heart in this season.

These kinds of moments are so precious to the Father and me as they led me into a time of direct and intentional conversation with Him. However, it didn't end there. This was the beginning of a great adventure that Father and I were going to undertake together. I had to leave everything behind and follow His call. It all began with a dream.

A few more days passed, and while I was in awe of what was happening, I still lived in a vulnerable place of pain and mistrust toward God. This was the paradox in this season. I would continue to desire everything I was experiencing, while I also needed the Father to guide me through the realities of burnout and mistrust of His character and His people. I had no idea where to go or what to do, or even what to believe about God at this point. Yet, I knew I was willing and able to follow His presence with diligence.

One night I went to bed unprepared for what was going to happen and had a dream that remains vivid in my mind today. I dreamt that I was falling into a pit. As I fell, witches were flying around me, screaming,

"Don't you dare go to Byron Bay!" However, a lady named Helena, whom I had never met and only heard of through a friend, sat by silently. When I woke up, I contacted my friend who knew Helena. At this point, I had not heard of or known what Helena was all about, but as it turned out, she had an excellent reputation in prayer ministry and a powerful prophetic gift.

Within a few hours I was on the phone with Helena, and as she began to speak I was on my back again and in the presence of God authentically and tangibly. As she began to prophesy, the prophetic target seemed to be my next season in life. To my surprise, after Helena was done, I was covered once again in gold dust.

What she said will remain with me all my days. However, I do not feel the need to share it here due to its value to me as a personal moment with God. It was a direct and pure connection that the Father had set up to speak to me, and the word was to go to Bryon Bay!

This solidified my resolve, and needless to say, within weeks, I had sold everything I owned, packed myself up, and moved to Byron Bay.

Papa was once again pursuing me relentlessly. He wanted me to be free and was willing to disrupt my world to achieve His goal of freedom in my life.

Romans 8:20-21

For the creation was subjected to futility, not willingly, but because of him who subjected it, in the hope that the creation itself will be set free from its bondage to corruption and obtain the freedom of the glory of the children of God.

He was calling me into His embrace, and I was ready to come. In this season, the revelation that God was giving me would lead me to become fully myself. It was an invitation to fully be seen in the mess of my life. Unfortunately God had not equipped the community I was a part of for the entirety of my brokenness and hiding from God and people was no longer an option. Brennan Manning makes a great point when he pens this thought in his book, 'Abbas Child.'

> *"In a futile attempt to erase our past, we deprive the community of our healing gift. If we conceal our wounds from fear and shame, our inner darkness can neither be illuminated nor become a light for others."*

-Brennan Manning-

During this season, I learned how to be open. I couldn't and dang well shouldn't expect vulnerability with God while hiding my true self from others. How could I possibly embrace the Love of God for myself while hiding what I had decided was unlovable from my peers? The only authentic way to love yourself is to let others love you; the authentic you. Not the polished and determined to be
accepted you. The vulnerable, genuine, and authentic you that only you know and only you can empower to feel loved.

We have all hidden the realities of our pain and struggle from each other. I could no longer tolerate this in my life. At this point, I feel I need to place a disclaimer; this reality without wisdom is detrimental to you and others around you. One thing I wish I had done before learning this was prepare those I trusted around me for the mess. I encourage you to do this better than I did; there is no need to lose relationships in this revelation. Prepare your friends and family for the journey, and make sure you articulate it well so they can be a support in your growth. In my learning and journey, I would be brash, rude, and honest in the name of transparency and vulnerability, all while expecting grace. There is a fine line between being transparent and being abusive. Make sure you walk it diligently; I lost many friends in my immaturity.

There is something so powerful about not being able to hide your mess. I will share more about the season up in Byron later, but for now, let's take a look at empowering ourselves not to hide. This is where we find paying attention to our motives to be invaluable. When we live authentically and vulnerably before others, we get to walk free of the things that hinder us in our hiddenness.

Let me share with you the truth about hiding,

When we have dealt with the core of our shame, only then will sin become powerless. For at the heart of sin lies the truth of shame.

It is my main desire to find where we stand with our Father. I do not want to do this in the sense of our position with God through purity or righteousness. At the core of one's identity there is a question that is driven by human curiosity. Who Is God and who does He say I am?

In the journey to understanding our intimate belonging, just what is it that God expects from us? To become hidden from love is the product of shame. We see this in the Garden of Eden and have for all time since. Adam and Eve become deceived by the serpent, we all know the story. The Father walks through the garden pining for his creation with a sense of loss and despair. This is where we see these words penned in the book of Genesis.

Genesis 3:12

"But the Lord God called to the man and said to him, "'Where are you?" And he said, "I heard the sound of you in the garden, and I was afraid because I was naked, and I hid."

Isn't it interesting that the first response to His Father in a position of deception was to hide? Remember that at this point, sin was not a thing. If we can, for a moment, translate this behaviour into our modern culture of Christianity we would see this same response of hiding is riddled throughout the church; a religion of performance Christianity without any reality to do with our holistic health. We have been taught that vulnerability looks like weakness. I am so glad to see what the Father is doing in the restoration of openness and vulnerability across the body of believers. As I mentioned in chapter one, the beginning of religious performance was modelled on my need to be seen and heard. I was not even aware of religion in and of itself, but the religious spirit is rife in this world. It has been preventing people from seeing their value, and I was one of its victims.

We hide from the reality of pure love because we struggle to trust it. I also touched on this in chapter one, but here I would like to engage with it a little more closely.

We need to become influential people in stepping into the possibility of receiving rejection. But please, for the Love of God, stop hiding from everyone and God whilst continuing to wonder why you don't feel valued. The key here is to take responsibility for your feelings. A great question I have learned to ask myself when seeking out whether my feelings are valid or not is this: "What is the relational cost of me engaging with this thought or feeling?" If it looks like engaging with the emotion will end in losing a relationship, I want to suggest that you are not partnering with the mind or the spirit of Christ! There is no biblical precedent for the idea of cutting off a relationship entirely with someone. Instead, I would say that we are responsible in all situations of relational breakdown, whether we are the victims or the perpetrator, to pursue restoration.

I know what this provokes in you; even as I type this out. I am convicted of approaching unavoidable relational breakdowns in my world. I have been a victim and a perpetrator of emotional and spiritual abuse in my short time on this healing journey. The lesson in not negating your emotion and empowering an abuser while still loving them is an ongoing battle. God has grace for where you are at in this. There is one thing I know; if we can cure this need to hide from love, then we will be able to empower others to step out of their darkness and retake control of their lives. This is purely trusting God for your determined value and not hinging it on the acceptance of others.

We have managed to implement the first sign of disbelief in God's Love toward us into our ministries by allowing our hidden shame to dictate the terms of our relationship with God and others. But unfortunately this will never allow our mess to be seen, and therefore we will never honestly deal with its effects on our lives and the lives of those around us.

Paul, the great apostle, put it like this.

Thinking more than we ought of ourselves
(Romans 12:3)

When we present ourselves differently from others, the people who follow us end up trying to aspire to a goal that we have not even achieved ourselves. When we present perfection without connection to those who look to us for guidance, what we perpetuate is hopelessness. I can't count the number of times I have asked a leader in my ignorance of this reality, "How do you live the way you live?" Looking back, I now realise why I never truly got an answer. The question itself probably sparked shame in those I asked. They were maybe struggling with the same thing I was. They may never have felt they could express in truth and lead well while being authentic in the reality that this is a journey of relentless self-discovery, and we need to apply grace for the journey.

This is deception at its finest. Although mostly unintentional, using the very beginning of sin, which, in reality, is simply put, "hiding." We have created an unspoken ministry rule that we can't possibly be vulnerable with our people or, more importantly, our friends. There cannot be a time for sharing our mess because we have to lead our congregations in the ways of righteousness.

We call it wisdom! While in fact, we trap everyone else in the same prison, which is the original deception.

We all struggle silently while we feel fake in our hiddenness. We do this while living out this life as an impostor, internally screaming for freedom from ourselves whilst presenting perfection. When we do this as a leader, people are made to feel hopeless.

We often do this because of our inability to value ourselves enough to seek help. It is insanity, and we see Jesus tackle this mentality in scripture.

In our impostor state or our act, we all fall into this category at some point in our journey. But remember, we need to carry grace for ourselves in this journey.

Matthew 23:27

"Woe to you, scribes and Pharisees, hypocrites! For you are like whitewashed tombs, which outwardly appear beautiful, but within are full of dead people's bones and all uncleanness. So you also outwardly appear righteous to others, but within you are full of hypocrisy and lawlessness.

Here we find a beautiful invitation of freedom from the pharisaical way of life. It is as if Jesus presents an opportunity for them, saying, "Guys, you don't have to pretend with me; I want to know you; just let me in."

Ultimately, remaining hidden looks like mistrust toward the loving nature that we believe God has for us. I want to share this thought with you from a book by Brennan Manning. This changed my life and it will help us as we take a moment to reflect on who we believe the Father is.

Facing our hiddenness looks like dealing with our misconceived beliefs about God and our value to Him.

Brennan said it best when he wrote this:

"Have you grappled with the core question of your faith, which is not 'is Jesus like God?' but 'Is God Jesus-like?' Do you comprehend that all the attitudes, values, qualities, and characteristics of my Son are mine, and he who sees Jesus sees me, His Father."

-Brennan Manning-

This is a question not for the faint-hearted. It's a question that will transform who you think the Father is. It will also help you drop your preconceived ideas and allow a new truth to wash over you. Perhaps one of the biggest deceptions occurred in the garden, and Adam's rebellion was maybe more than just not doing what God had told him to do and eat from the tree.

The painful truth is this: perhaps to "The Father", the most significant pain was not our rebellion, but instead this wound of rejection inflicted by us as He came running toward us in restoration. We remained in our place of disconnection by our own free will, Not because of a behaviour but instead we changed our belief.

Is it too much to believe that God is so relational that He would be affected by our actions or perhaps even hurt? After all He had done, after all the goodness and love that He had shared, Adam and Eve still did not trust His goodness toward them. We still struggle with this truth after all the natural manifestations in the garden and all the living proof of His heart toward us. We still allow our own decision to hide from Him to rob us of who He is and whom He says we are.

This has not changed since the garden. Post the cross; we still struggle to accept who we are to Him, and worse, to accept His Love, even after He laid down His life for us to be restored to our position as sons. It is this relational view that will make God real to us. I am tired of talking about my greatest love as if He died on the cross without rising, like He is a mere distant thought.

I am not trying to add to the scripture. I'm just simply tapping into the despair the Father feels when I hide from him, as if He cries out, "When will you believe I love you? Will you allow this to affect you? Or will it pass you by as another story and not the truth?"

My heart is broken for Him in my neglect, to be honest with my ever-present Papa. Let me leave you with one last thought. I want to share a scripture with you; one last "hurrah" on the result of hiddenness.

Matthew 7:22

"Not everyone who says to me, 'Lord, Lord,' will enter the kingdom of heaven, but the one who does the will of my Father who is in heaven. On that day, many will say to me, 'Lord, Lord, did we not prophesy in your name, and cast out demons in your name, and do many mighty works in your name?' And then will I declare to them, 'I never knew you; depart from me, you workers of lawlessness" '

Let us focus for a second on the severity of this scripture, look solely at Jesus' response to those who did great exploits without being known to God. You see, we have made our ministry all about the pursuit of understanding God without being known by Him.

I ask you this: does God know you? Have you opened your life to Him in reality? Or do you believe that He is a dictator who does not need to know you and instead He is merely the fulfiller of all your needs? Have you ever been in a relationship like this? How tiring is it? The perpetual cycles of self-fulfilling sorrow never appease your emotional abuser, and in this case your abuser is you. Does God know you? Are you still hiding in your shame while striving to feel acceptance? Are you a place of rest for the Holy Spirit, a personal friend and a refuge?

These are some of the most challenging questions Christians can ask themselves, "Do I know God and am I known to God?" The beauty of these two questions lies in the Father's excitement when we ask them.

Be honest with Him for a minute, but don't do it if you are not prepared for the journey that comes with it.

Let's pray.
Father; even as I type this, my very own hypocrisy challenges the core of my hidden state that I would not respond as the first Adam to your calls of desire for deep intimacy with me. Here I am, a prodigal surviving on the scraps of affection I give to you, coming to the end of myself, puffing my chest out on the profound and long journey home. Help me to believe, as I embark on this journey, that you would receive me as a son who desires to be known by you. Father, I think the answer to the question in my heart of what you expect from me is merely to respond to your voice in the garden, "Adam, where are you? I can't feel you".
Father, I'm here, and I am yours!
Amen.

The Journey

THE STORY OF JUDGMENT

After discussing the 'harm in hiding' I think it is essential to know and understand how to live this out without judging those who are not living in this freedom yet. In reality, understanding God's nature will release you into the ability to be transparent and vulnerable. One of the hardest things I experienced in this is that this freedom will not sit well with everyone! It is essential to know that you may feel like you are around people who don't 'get you'. A mistake I made throughout this journey was that I thought that I had a great awakening and began to treat people like I was living in a deeper level of understanding. I lost all patience and grace for those on their own journey. I was living in judgment of people's inability to be genuine while my behaviour was offering them a reason to feel unsafe around me.

The interesting thing I have found about judgment in my own life is that it has an ability to become a filter in how I look at situations. I could be looking at the truth, but my misguided opinion of the situation would end up concocting a far more sinister reality. Living in this place of judgment is the birthplace of relational conspiracy; which looks like living a lifestyle that thinks that everyone is out to get me based on my perception of their intentions. Without wisdom while we are walking on a journey toward freedom from hiding, we will often feel exposed and get hurt. It is critical to keep yourself in check and not let the feeling of isolation that can come from feeling misunderstood rule our inner life.

Living in judgment produced one of the hardest and darkest years of my life. I was living in the fruit of my preconceptions and relational conspiracies. I have to say that even in the moments that my judgments proved right I had to learn that celebrating being right at the cost of a relationship was not at all healthy. Of course, you can still walk in judgment and be right. But, for the most part, judgment is a posture of the heart that is steeped in pride and has no place in the Christian journey.

I experienced this reality and the cost of judgment for the short time I lived in Byron Bay. I feel that telling the extent of this story would be dishonoring to the re-established relationships that have been formed in restoration. In short, I was misrepresented, which led to being misunderstood and then I fought my way through the year holding onto my anger as if it were a tool that would help me see victory. Unfortunately when I could have sought freedom from all the pain in the early stages of this relational breakdown I decided to look for justice instead of understanding.

This is the main issue we find when we sit on the seat that was designed for God. If I am honest, parts of me still want justice, but no longer at the cost of God's mercy, and certainly not at the expense of relationships. If the cost of your justice is a relational breakdown, you are likely not in line with how God views the situation you have judged. The first thing I will say about this topic is that it always has two people's sense of pride wrapped up in a desire to be correct. Two people's needs to alleviate the shame of being wrong. Usually, when it comes to it, pride and shame are at the centre of any, and in my opinion, every relational breakdown.

Let me share a secret with you! Whether you are right or wrong, in a relational breakdown you have stood on your pride to be so, and this will cause communication pollution. Would it be too wrong of us to decide, even in being right, to lay it all down for relational restoration?

"Imagine with me for a second, if Jesus on the cross and instead of crying out, "Forgive them, for they know not what they do," He said, "Father, they have hurt me, and I deserve justice."

As hard as it is for me to admit, justice should not be in the vocabulary of faith-filled Christians in the context of our relationships. We should always be the first to extend restoration in laying down our rights to be correct. When fear of exposure drives our interior, it is detrimental to approach confrontation, when our drive is self- protection or self preservation we know that It is only going to lead to a fruit that is of the flesh. We need to become people who realise that making a mistake and being wrong does not mean we are worthless. We could say that the easiest way to find out if your self-worth lays in the hands of God or in the hands of man is in the realm of your ability to admit fault without it robbing you of your peace.

This is a courageous lifestyle and an invitation to become better at being like Jesus. Perhaps one of the biggest traps of judgment is that in it, you feel a sense of vindication. Often in this there is a need being met in you and it is usually fueled by our flesh and void of Spirit. It would do you an excellent service to understand that having a need met is not always a good thing, and in this need based justice there is an emotional trap for you. It is confronting to think that the sense of justice you achieved and that felt so good was actually brought through an ungodly method. In these acts of judgment we become trapped in bitterness and miss the heart of the Father. We end up actually having faith in our ability to find Justice instead of trusting God's intent to mold us even more into His likeness. Imagine if we choose to take opportunities to restore people instead of judging them. This would empower those that hurt us to change and also empower us to love on a deeper and more Christ-like level.

To become truly one in Christ, we need to submit to our accusers in the same way that Jesus did and free them in love. I often forget that the same Holy Spirit that has done work in me is in everyone else. I try desperately to stand in His position of showing people what they need to learn. I quickly forget that my learning was a work of grace that led me to freedom.

Hebrews 12:15

See to it that no one fails to obtain the grace of God; that no "root of bitterness" springs up and causes trouble, and by it, many become defiled;

Let's hammer this home for a second. The scripture says, "See to it that NO ONE fails to obtain the grace of God." This is a request to make sure that we extend grace to keep people's hearts free from bitterness. This is our responsibility to love.

After all, the scripture is clear.

Matthew 5:24-26

Leave your gift there before the altar and go. First, be reconciled to your brother, and then come and offer your gift.

Come to terms quickly with your accuser while you are going with him to court, lest your accuser hand you over to the judge, and the judge to the guard, and you be put in prison.

Truly, I say to you, you will never get out until you have paid the last penny.

It would benefit all of us if we held this intention in our relationships. Our right to be right is less valuable than our need for each other.

We need to position ourselves for reconciliation. Our pride in being right and the wound to our pride when we have been found to be wrong robs us of our desire to be connected.

Yes, you have the power to inflict a deeper wound of shame in relationships or alleviate it with an unmerited experience of grace. I know it does not seem fair, but what if you are the healing they need and the acceptance they have never experienced. Your actions amidst your pain could serve God's purpose in someone's life, and your response could be the healing factor for their breakthrough. Heaping hot coals of love on their head that leads to repentance is a guilt-free justice. It will empower you to love them in and through their mess like you have always desired to be loved. Hopefully, this will set them free from themselves and lead to conviction and change but this can not be our motive. We need to stay focused on the growth that is happening in us, not the one we think everyone else needs.

This should provoke in you a sense of excitement because it will lead you to a deeper freedom. The uncomfortable part of this is your flesh trying to justify holding on to the bitterness, and if there's a sense of enthusiasm in your spirit, it is because it will be jumping at the potential freedom you could have. The choice is always yours, and there is grace on the journey for you.

Before I go on, I want to express that in no way am I saying that if you have experienced abuse that it was okay. It wasn't, and if that is you, then I am deeply sorry for what took place. I know the Father is hurting with you. What I am saying is that holding onto the hurt isn't helping you.

We want people to admit their shortcomings and failures because it feeds our need for superiority. This is founded in a godless culture that has based its success on being dominant instead of loving.

God's justice always looks like mercy, and ours almost always desires exposure.

Whether you are wrong or right in the midst of relational confrontation, God's position is always in reconciliation and this is the posture we must take. If we can grasp this, the prize for us is that we will become free from bitterness and broken relationships. We all have the power to free someone, and we have the power to bind them also. Even today, you hold the key to unlocking someone from the chains of your bitterness. In a sense, we have held hearts at ransom through judgment, thinking it affects them. People don't even know how or why they hurt us most of the time. So it isn't worth holding onto the offense, even if you are right.

For me it was not an entirely spiritual journey of discovery. There was an aspect of my will that had to change. I needed to learn how to love without a price tag and that was painful. I quickly began to realise that if there were ever a cost to love, it would look like death to the need I carried in my flesh.

Throughout this season in Byron, I held my accusers accountable for what was happening in my life and was motivated by the idea of them being exposed. I would intentionally stand in the way of reconciliation to find my justice while waiting for them to become exposed in their behaviour. But unfortunately, I was on the journey toward my own exposure. I was angry and I desperately wanted to shut them down. I didn't understand that this kind of thinking deepened the cycle of my brokenness and left me blinded.

When we can't see the people any longer, and we only see their behaviours, we have lost sight of the heart of Jesus. True love keeps no record of wrong.

1 Corinthians 13:7

Love bears all things, believes all things, hopes all things, and endures all things.

It was safe to say that I was not even close to bearing, hoping, and enduring in love at this stage of my life. It came at a time when the Father spoke clearly to me in this season, "Adam, My justice and your justice look very different." This conversation changed everything.

As I pondered on this for a while within the context of the revelation of the Father's heart, I was quietly reminded that I am to replicate the life of Christ here on earth. This led me to delve into what God's justice looked like in conjunction with my sin.

I soon realised that I would be in a heap of trouble if God's justice looked anything like how mine was manifesting. What I had determined justice to be didn't line up with Jesus's actions, which was deeply troubling to me.

In the garden of Gethsemane we see a justice that does not look fair at all. Our Jesus, pure and sinless was led to a cross in sacrifice to bring us all mercy. In His humanity, we see him cry out for another way, and then He, the God we all serve and love has to be strengthened by an angel. I took away a few realities from this. Firstly, I realised that I had believed that God did not value how I was feeling because he was still blessing the perpetrators of my pain. I have since found that it is okay to talk to the Father about how we are experiencing injustice. We can get so caught up on what we should and shouldn't say to Him that we forget that all the while that He knows our innermost parts.

Gary Morgan, one of today's most influential prophetic voices, tells a great story about those who have hurt us getting blessed. He explains that he went through a season of frustration watching people who have hurt him get blessed. When he asked the Lord why this was happening, he heard the Lord speak to him, "I am blessing them because you won't!" It is so important to keep a spirit of blessing because it is the nature of Jesus!

We have a significant amount of understanding of what we inherit as sons through Christ regarding all the benefits, signs, wonders and financial blessings. These are great realities. However, we often don't stop to implement some of the behaviours that we are called to as sons of God. I want to say that we have inherited a far more profound reality in Jesus than things we can merely receive. In Jesus, we have gained an astounding ability to give gifts of forgiveness and redemption to those in our lives who haven't offered it in return. The journey of sonship is one of sacrifice on earth; we now represent the Father and His kingdom. To the world, our representation is a presentation of the Father and therefore we must free ourselves from things like judgment.

Our Father, in His wisdom, decided not to hold our wrongs against us and His justice looked like a release to empower us in mercy and grace. Even when he was the one we perpetrated rejection toward, He pursued us in Jesus. This is so incredible and a great picture of how we are designed for connection to Him as well as to each other.

We have been given a gift that we are expected to provide for the world around us. Grace and mercy don't just stop at us receiving it from God. In reality, this is where it begins, and we are called to pay it forward.

So why do we hold our offenders in an emotional prison for their behaviour?

I would like to suggest as a thought that how we treat others amid their sin and how we react to their repentance is how we view the Father and His response to us.

We tend to replicate to one another what we believe. If I believe God is a God who will punish my behaviour then that is the view I will offer to those around me. When it comes to the symptoms of sin (being our behaviours), we must understand the root in order for us to be able to deal with them correctly. We must understand the sickness we have in order to figure out how to treat it.

The best example of this is the story of two people who are very dear to my heart. I received a video call from this young couple at work one day. As we were chatting away, all seemed well but I felt that some news was coming. Eventually, I mustered up the courage, choosing to trust my discernment and asked, "So what's up, guys? What's wrong?"

My friend's voice dropped considerably and his girlfriend looked away as shame reared its ugly head. Then he looked at me and began to tell me how they were pregnant outside of marriage with a shame-filled voice.

At this point, I remember sitting there and all these feelings came flooding into my mind, "They need to get their stuff together; I'm so disappointed and angry with you." What was I going to say to them? This went on for what felt like ten minutes of silence, but in reality, it had only been a few seconds until I heard God speak, "Adam, tell them they are not having a shame baby."

What was incredible about this was the instant change I witnessed in their demeanour as I looked to my friend's partner and relayed the message that the Lord had spoken. Immediately, the conversation went from sadness to celebration. The Father was not empowering their mistake, but He restored their view of their position in His eyes.

All my initial reactions and thoughts were about how I would treat myself in failure. What I would deem the Father's response to my sin was very different from how we would see Jesus respond. I was operating in judgment and not mercy. I would have made my view of Him their problem. I wonder if you can think of a time that this was true for you? Where, instead of expressing the truth of God's nature to someone, you let your own self- loathing beliefs dictate the terms of their freedom.

On the other end of this moment was my friends need to feel condemned or ashamed to be able to feel and receive the love and forgiveness of God. We have a clause in our subconscious state that says we can only accept pure love but only after paying the price that we feel we deserve. We beg to be forgiven so that we can feel free from our shame. We act as if the Father is dangling a carrot of forgiveness that leads to a freedom that He has already won for us.

To kill this reality in our lives we do not need to look any further than the Father's response to the son in the prodigal story. The son concocts his plea, "Father, I am not worthy of being a son; please just allow me to be a servant in your house." The Father's response should cause a deep search in us. He overlooks his son's repentance which is veiled self-loathing and restores him instantly.

In our self-loathing statements that usually begin sounding like, "Father, we are not worthy," He meets us with a ring and a robe and restores us to the position we held before we walked away.

We have to stop transferring our disbelief in His goodness onto each other.

Thankfully before I offered my friends what I felt I deserved in my own sin God intervened. When the words fumbled out of my mouth, "You do not have a shame baby," it was as if we all felt empowered to break the cycle of behaviour based on our misconception of His character.

This led me to a new understanding, and it blew my mind. So what is a sin if it is not founded on the mindset of bad behaviour? In the Old Testament we have the law or commands that we have used as guidelines to live in an acceptable way to God.

These laws are what I would call behavioural requirements, but as we know through the coming of Christ God knew that we could not live up to the standard. So He sent His Son Jesus, the only one who could. This established a new spiritual law, one of freedom, not captivity.

Galatians 3:23-24

Now before faith came, we were held captive under the law, imprisoned until the coming faith would be revealed. So then, the law was our guardian until Christ came, in order that we might be justified by faith.

We needed a new covenant, and a new agreement leads to a redefining of the requirements around our behaviour and sin. Look carefully at this; it is the key to joining Christ in a transformational relationship. It will change your thoughts in becoming like Christ. You will no longer need to feel you have to become holy and righteous because you will believe you have these realities in true relationship with Him. It is in the being and not the becoming that we find our freedom.

The old revelation of behavioural sin has been made obsolete.

Hebrews 8:13

In speaking of a new covenant, he makes the first one obsolete. And what is becoming obsolete and growing old is ready to vanish away.

So, this leaves us in no man's land when it comes to sin. Let's look at what we know through the person of Christ. We know that He died for the world's sins, not just for those who believe.

1 John 2:2

He is the propitiation for our sins, not for ours only but the sins of the whole world.

And it is important to follow on with why He did this.

1 John 2:3

and by this, we know that we have come to know him if we keep his commandments.

He became our sin for two reasons; firstly, so we could know Him. This is powerful because He did this so we could understand and see His nature towards our rebellion while we were still His enemies. He was trying to correct our view of Him. Secondly, He came to help us keep His commandments. Well, that is not very clear. Didn't Jesus make those old things obsolete?

Let us look at how sin is defined in the new covenant.

1 John 3:4

Everyone who makes a practice of sinning also practices lawlessness; sin is lawlessness.

Making a practice of sinning is lawlessness, and while the old law is obsolete, a new law has been established. So, there is still a requirement to live up to. If it is not behavioural, then what is it? And why should we change? At this point, I would like to make it clear that I am not condoning a lifestyle that does not replicate holiness. Please read on; I will explain myself.

John 13:34

a new commandment I give to you, that you love one another: just as I have loved you, you also are to love one another.

The new law in Christ is Love. He takes us from "You must do" to "I have done, so you are." But this is only achieved in a relational context.

Here's the thing, we have made the absolution of sin the salvation point, and I am afraid we may have got this wrong. The salvation point is and has always been in relationship. We accept in faith that God is who He says He is. It was shame that stole this faith from us in the garden, and it is still what keeps us from His nature today.

Romans 6:15-23

What then? Are we to sin because we are not under law but under grace? By no means!

Let me say this: grace is a covering for our behavioural sin. But, due to the new covenant definition of sin (the law of love), we need to love God. This transforms us, and our desires become His desires. God is not offended by our behavioural sin, but the fruit of knowing love transforms us from desiring sin to desiring love. We don't change
because we have to; we change because we have fallen in love. Perhaps a great example in a simple context would be this: Remember the moment you met that girl or boy you are now married to, you wanted to please them in every way? You didn't have to; it was just a natural response to a pure connection with love.

Verse 16

Do you not know that if you present yourself to anyone as obedient slaves, you are slaves of the one you obey, either of sin, which leads to death, or obedience, which leads to righteousness?

If you don't place sin in its correct context, you will be a slave to its definition. This will either make or break your connection with the Father.

Hey, don't take my word for it. Spend some time talking intimately With Him; He loves to speak to you.

Verse 17,

But thanks be to God, that you who were once slaves of sin have become obedient from the heart to the standard of teaching to which you were committed and, having been set free from sin, have become slaves of righteousness.

Verse 18 - 19

I am speaking in human terms, because of your natural limitations. Just as you once presented your members as slaves to impurity and lawlessness, leading to more lawlessness, now present your members as slaves to righteousness, leading to sanctification. For when you were slaves of sin, you were free in regard to righteousness.

This is a statement that you should allow to wash over you today.

Verse 20-23

But what fruit were you getting at that time from the things of which you are now ashamed? For the end of those things is death. But now that you have been set free from sin and have become slaves of God, the fruit you get leads to sanctification and its end, eternal life. For the wages of sin is death, but the free gift of God is eternal life in Christ Jesus our Lord.

In conclusion, we need to free ourselves from our predetermined ideas on sin and separation. The idea that our Father would create something in us as a default that separates us from Him is ludicrous. Sin is no longer a behavioural issue; it is a relational one. Love the Lord your God with all your heart! This will transform you. Until then you have mercy and grace through faith.

Once we rectify how we believe God responds to us, we are empowered to set each other free from our prisons of bondage.

Judgment is the product of our misconceived right to punish others and ourselves for being flawed. Jesus does not do this. What He does is quite the opposite. We serve a God who has modeled how to live a life forsaken to the idea of truly loving others. We are not designed to be lone rangers in this journey of faith. The old African proverb states, "It takes a village to raise a child." This reality is true of faith. It takes a community, leadership, and guidance with counsel to raise a son and if we keep bucking against people's love for us based on our judgments we will never find the freedom in which we are called to live.

For me, as someone who has a list longer than you can imagine of church wounding, I have never given up on the bride of Christ. People often wound us, and the reality is that we can only be healed through the very thing that has hurt us. In the next chapter, I will tackle the story of friendship and what it looks like to lay down your life for your brother or sister and live in healthy communion.

Let's pray: Father, help me release the people attached to the offense I have chosen. I choose to bless them and forgive them and take away the power they have had in my life by releasing my bitterness towards them. Help me get free from my need to have justice, Lord, and seek your justice over my own. I love you, Father, and I want to fall deeply in love with you so I can be an accurate representation of you here on earth! Then, your will be done; your kingdom come.

The Journey

THE STORY OF FRIENDSHIP

I want to share my journey to understanding how to become a true friend with you. This is a lesson in patience, honour, and faith in those God has placed around me. It has been truly humbling. And when I mention humility, I don't mean it in its most common sense. The false one where you say everything good about you was all God, and you are just a mere vessel for his achievement.

No, this isn't what humility looks like. I mean it in its truest sense. Humility toward the Father looks like a willful submission to His call on your life. It is becoming who you are meant to be, which can look pretty amazing.

I want you to change your mind on humility because if you cannot celebrate or love yourself, then I must ask, how do you expect that you will be able to let anyone in on a deep enough level to love and celebrate you truly?

True humility toward one another looks like helping this reality of self-love come to fruition in each other's lives, this has to happen despite our fears and self-loathing thoughts. We begin the journey of abandoning our desire for safety by being humble enough to put our friend's need for freedom before our own.

We need to change our approach to humility when we step into the realm of friendship because if we are honest, we have used it as a pretty darn good excuse not to celebrate ourselves. Usually, this has been out of fear of our peers, ensuring that we don't get ahead of ourselves and begin to think more than we ought of ourselves.

What I faced on my journey of friendship, and began to perpetuate, is what we call 'tall poppy syndrome' here in Australia. Until recently, I never felt I fully allowed myself to become who I wanted to become, or more alarmingly, to fulfil who I was called to be. The reasons are not entirely clear as to why this happens. However, in my experience, whenever I mustered up enough courage to pop my head up over the fence of success, there was always somebody there to stop me from believing in myself. When people came with their unwelcomed opinions, my personal view of myself simply submitted to their doubt and began to partner with it.

This is truly one of the most profound realisations I had to have within myself. The truth is, I was not only someone who was a victim of this culture, but I also was a perpetrator. The cycle of needing to justify my failure through seeing others fail was, and is, the most toxic thing I believe we have in our culture here in Australia. Perhaps it is even worse than seeing this mentality and culture riddled within our churches under the concealed need to compete. To be seen as anointed.

To be honest, I would say that our motivation for this is pure. This is what makes it so hard to see how damaging it is. Simply put, we are motivated by a need in our design to be seen as significant to someone on a deep and relatable level. This is seldom intentional but a naturally internal drive that has had dysfunction attached to it since the fall.

Perhaps this just applies to me. I am not suggesting that everyone falls into this category. However, I am trying to express to you my reality in the hope that you can begin to be honest enough with yourself to find what is needed to be transformed so that your relationships can better represent Christ. After all, the scripture tells us that they will know us by how we love one another, and the gravity of that scripture is often skipped over.

In my evangelism experience, I have seen people completely transformed by witnessing this kind of radical and pure love played out in our community. Let me ask you a simple but unfortunate question. Is the church known for its love for one another? This is perhaps one of the most painful realisations that we need to face. Currently, we are known for the issues in society that we stand for or against. The church has planted its feet firmly in the realm of judgment on political decisions and peoples' struggles.

John 13:34-35

A new commandment I give to you, that you love one another: just as I have loved you, you also are to love one another.

By this, all people will know that you are my disciples if you have a love for one another."

The world will discover the reality of God through seeing us have a love for one another, and they will know that we are one of His people through this. Straying away from friendship for a second, let's look at this concept in the realm of the church.

This is something we all need to begin to consider if we want to see revival happen. So often, as leaders, we are too busy trying to prove the anointing on our lives and how our expression of God is the most valid. We need to understand that alone, we cannot house revival. The Evangelicals need the Pentecostals and vice versa. The lost art of love has fallen by the wayside in our need for self-promotion. The only result of this has been broken relational experiences that have led to christian division. I have experienced the isolation of this spiritual competitiveness that I am expressing on a deeply personal level.

For a long time, I feared the opinions of others when it came to pursuing what I felt God was calling me into. Friends would often say, "I don't think you are called to this.

In one instance, I was even told I had no anointing by a leader I looked up to. This culture of diminishing each other's purpose was left unchallenged in my life, and it was the cause of a deep shut down in me that could have completely stolen my ability to achieve all that God has for me.

These kinds of experiences led me into the trap of saying and believing things like, "I don't care what people think of me." At first thought, this statement would seem sound, as though I have been freed from the shackles of man-made opinion. However, I would like to suggest that this is a trap and an anti-God mentality. If we don't care what people think about us, we are making a statement that people and their opinions are of no value to us, and this is not the mind of Christ. I would say that I landed here in a relationship for a time because it felt like a safe way to protect my heart. But, in reality, it was another mechanism for me to tell people to stay away.

I suggest we repent if we have lived this kind of Godless attitude as friends and as denominations. We are called as children of God to represent a God who paid the ultimate price for people to be connected with Him. The cost of loving those in the world is a pittance next to that of our Christ and His cross. We need to mature in this because it is literally how the world will find out that Christ is the only one who can fill the void in their hearts.

Thankfully, in all these experiences with people, I had the evidence of my story locked up in the people who helped me walk through it. These were some of the most painful experiences with people I have ever had, and I am sure there will be more. However, I want to encourage you that there is strength in loving relentlessly - even loving your abusers. I know it is counterintuitive, I know it hurts, and I know that there is grace for the process of anger and your need for justice. I don't want to devalue your pain, but I want to help you see how moving past it can have an eternal impact on relationships.

Being questioned on who I was at my core and being told that people didn't think I was honest with my story could have wiped me out altogether. At this stage in my life, I had no solid foundational value of myself at all.

I am blessed and truly thankful to God that He continued to woo me into His presence and helped me find a way to love at all costs. After more than a decade I am still on this journey, and I still have a lot to learn, but I will always choose to love, even when it hurts.

At this point in my life, I wish I had understood what sowing the seeds of judgment was going to inevitably produce in my relationships. Understanding the sowing and reaping principle surrounding this would have saved me a lot of trouble. Instead, I began the process of reaping what I had sown as I transferred these experiences of judgment and pain into my Christian journey.

Eventually I began to inflict the same traumatic experiences onto those who were looking to me for answers. It is interesting when you see bitterness literally begin to defile "the many" as is described in Hebrews. I had a massive chip on my shoulder and it manifested itself in a way that sounded something like this."This is what I went through, so you must have the same experiences to learn the same lessons and inevitably find your revelation to walk through it." I wasn't offering them help. I expected that they had to walk through the same hardships that I did because it somehow would make sense of my pain. And the basis of this was that I couldn't share my mistakes with them because I would likely lose their respect. For me, this was meeting an ungodly need to feel superior and somehow reconcile my personal experiences.

We tend to look at what we see in the flesh and then talk others out of their dreams. We mask this with a pure motive of self-protection when all we're doing is projecting our views and inner fears onto those who are daring to dream with God. We're stuck in our self-doubt, and we offer it to our friends as if to say we are doing them a favour.

Don't dream because then I may have to." Once this fear sets in, we need to find its root. For many of us, that's typically found in our desire to be accepted. My need to be accepted had been firmly wrapped up in my story, a story I had placed all my value in, and it cost me a fortune in relational equity over the years.

The reality is that tall poppy syndrome is best described as an attempt to feel at least equal or better than those around us. We love the underdog here in Australia, but as soon as he gets on an even playing field, we try to remind him of all his faults until he stops trying to surpass our own achievements.

I have manifested this tall poppy syndrome behaviour in my life throughout various times. But I want to highlight one personal story that may paint the picture of why this is so important to dismantle in our lives. Before I do, it's essential to know that the tall poppy is not only subject to Australians; it is rife in most British settlements worldwide. Suppose you resonate with this kind of story. In that case, the best cause of action is to approach the issue with transparency, never making your emotional state the problem of others, but owning your end and not expecting an apology in return.

Here's the story I promised.

So, I discovered I had an issue with tall poppy syndrome when I met my friend, who, for privacy purposes, will remain nameless. At this point, I was helping with a largely successful young adults ministry in Adelaide, and I felt seen and made to be notable by my senior leaders. So, when this friend arrived on the scene, we connected instantly. We were like-minded and passionate, but as soon as he began to be noticed by the leadership, I witnessed behaviour that I did not like. I was no longer the alpha, and I began to compete.

I was willing to help him get established in the church, but as soon as he was, I hoped silently he would make mistakes so I would look better than he was. I want to clarify that I was not simply okay with this mentality. I struggled with its reality, and I would subconsciously decide to partner with it more often than not.

I could never champion him at all. When people would be amazed about what he said or whom he led on the streets to Jesus, I would meet it with many negatives. In the middle of all of this was the unfortunate truth that I would profess that he was one of my closest friends when people would ask.

Without knowing it, we would both proceed to pull the rug out from under each other's feet relationaly to hold a deeper connection than the other. We'd lead each other into bad situations where our shame would dictate the activities of the evening and then walk out repentant toward each other, vowing we would never share what we got up to in protection of each other. However, if we were given the opportunity or we were frustrated enough with each other at the time, we would expose each other to people we both had relationships with or respected in order to feel superior or more seen by those who held influence in our lives.

We wanted to be friends because we could see what knowing each other would do for our reputations, but it was a relationship founded on using each other to get connections. Have you ever had a relationship like this? It looks like starting a relationship with someone because they have something we want instead of simply wanting to know someone and be known for the sake of connection. Like me, I would wager that your motives were always very pure, at least on the surface. But, as soon as our need isn't met, we begin to sabotage or hurt the others involved because we feel a need for relational justice.

We do this to leaders all the time; I have often wondered why I extend more honour to a leader or a preacher than to the people who journey with me through life! God spoke to me about this one day, and I want to share it with you. It is a hard-hitting statement, but this is what He said.

"Adam, when you honour a stranger more than those close to you, it is simply idol worship." To be a good friend and journey our relationship well, we need to honour the people in our lives who walked with us into what we stand in. Countless times I abandoned those I was in a relationship with to spend time trying to be known by people I respected more than those who loved me. I have had to repent for this countless times over the years. The reality was that I was using leaders to further me in my journey of becoming a person of influence, and if they didn't fill my need they quickly became the enemy.

This will do you more damage than good. Trust me when I say God will open doors when He sees you loving well and doing relationships right.

Let's get back to the story of my friend in Adelaide. I often wonder what we could have achieved if we had worked together or had the maturity to see what was happening. Still, instead, we built more and more frustration which eventually led to an inevitable failure in friendship. Thankfully, I can say we are great friends and have a healthy relationship now, but learning through this has changed how I believe relationships should occur.

The residual effect of these kinds of relationships has been insecurity surrounding vulnerability toward people we are close with. However, the defining factor of change toward connection has to be our relentless pursuit of Jesus. Now whenever we are in the same place, we can catch up and connect over our love for Jesus instead of our deficiency in relationships. There is still work to be done, but we are getting there.

No genuine relationship is ever worth giving up on, in my opinion. But, in this case, my friend has seen the best of me and the worst of me, and that provides a pure foundation for going forward in a kingdom mindset that will change and impact many lives.

So how do we change this about ourselves and become a believer in people, go on to champion their visions, promote their dreams, and believe in them?

I will unpack a story of a man of God who didn't believe in what God had called him into. I intend to discover what we can achieve if we make a stand in championing one another despite what we see with our own eyes. You and I can achieve something powerful by having a community of believers around us.

Now, when I say believers, I am not talking about faith-filled belief, but instead, I am talking about personal believers in the dreams of others, like friends who lift you over your doubt and champion your call.

Many of us never get to experience people's faith in us genuinely. We could say that maybe we are reaping what we have sown concerning relationships. I speak for myself when I say this, as up until very recently, I would see another's success and would mostly feel jealousy, frustration, and envy instead of celebration, promotion, and belief.

I've been working hard to change this about myself, and for great reason. As I've begun to champion the dreams of others, I've found that my dreams have come to pass. A great biblical example of what we can achieve when our friends support us can be found in the Old Testament.

Let's take a look at the story of Jehu.

2 Kings 9:1-3

Then Elisha the prophet called one of the sons of the prophets and said to him, "Tie up your garments, take this flask of oil in your hand, and go to Ramoth-Gilead. And when you arrive, look there for Jehu, the son of Jehoshaphat, son of Nimshi. And go in and have him rise from among his fellows, and lead him to an inner chamber. Then take the flask of oil and pour it on his head and say, 'Thus says the Lord, I anoint you king over Israel.' Then open the door and flee; do not linger."

Jehu received a word in secret, one that made little sense. The word seemed to be one of rebellion, as Jehu served King Ahab as both a commander and a servant. Yet here he was in a position of calling, anointed in secret to become the next king of Israel. If I were in Jehu's place, I would have felt pretty nervous about stepping into this, but Jehu had some great friends. Let's read on.

2 Kings 9:11

When Jehu came out to the servants of his master, they said to him, "Is all well? Why did this mad fellow come to you?" And he said to them, "You know the fellow and his talk."

When he came out from this inner room dripping with oil and his men approached him, They instantly faced him with an opportunity to share the prophecy.

How many of us have received a prophecy and have had to face a comment like, "Yeah, but are they a prophet?" when sharing our excitement with friends? Or "I heard that person was wrong about this or that?" Or even perhaps, "That person is a mad man."

I am not sure why, maybe it was from embarrassment, but Jehu tossed the word by the wayside and said, "You know the fellow and his talk," instantly shutting the word down in his heart. This can be so detrimental.

How do we trust what our friends hear in secret? I have found that my mistrust in this has been founded on my experience with a person. We need to remember what God has taken us from to champion the unbelievable in others. In truth, mistrusting someone's experience with the Father is rooted in judgment and jealousy. We either judge them as unable or are jealous of their pursuit and ability. This is where tall poppy kicks in, and we curb their enthusiasm with what I like to call a wet blanket ministry! We dampen their flame out of our own insecurity.

I want to be a person who celebrates and dreams with them when faced with someone's word. Yet, in this circumstance, Jehu himself was shutting it down. Luckily for Jehu, his friends decided to dig deeper, and so should we. It just shows how careful we need to be with our language when dealing with the hearts of others.

2 Kings 9:12

And they said, "That is not true; tell us now."
And he said, "Thus and so he spoke to me,
saying, 'Thus says the Lord, I anoint you king
over Israel.'"

Imagine with me for a second (this shouldn't be too hard) you have a call and a gift in your life that you may have hidden under a bushel in fear of the response from friends, family, or even pastors.

But what would it look like for you if you had someone who walked with you and called you up to your giftings? I often hear from Christians that someone else is more gifted than they are or that they're not called to certain things.

If this is you, know that the truth is in you and stop hiding it from the world. In secret, you hope that you're of some worth to the kingdom, and the good news is that you are. You just need to believe it.

One of the best things about this reality of being championed is that it only comes to fruition in our lives when we sow that seed in someone else. I wouldn't blame you for thinking, "Adam, this is a romantic notion, but no one will champion me!" Let me mention that the most powerful way to produce something we need in our lives is to sow it into someone else's world. It would be best if you asked not who can champion you but who you can champion.

Jehu was a commander loved by his soldiers because he walked into battle with them, fought alongside them, and led in relationships. We can see in the following passage that, through what he had sown, his friends were willing to walk into anything for him and with him.

2 Kings 9:13

Then in haste, every man of them took his garment and put it under him on the bare steps, and they blew the trumpet and proclaimed, "Jehu is king."

Jehu's friends declared the word as truth over his life, and then he achieved what God had called him to do. They shared in his glory, and his victory was their victory.

I encourage you to abandon competition, strife, and gift-stifling behaviour and think of the big picture for the kingdom.

So back to the original question. How do we become a believer in people? It looks like choosing to lay down our desire to be unique and see what is in each other. We must look to the reality that our Christian brother's success is our Father's success, and we love at all costs.

If we did this, we would be called into faith in our calling on a much deeper level than ever before. Instead of relying on our gifts and view of ourselves to establish our ministries and impact, we could trust what everyone else has expressed about us regarding our intrinsic value to the kingdom. What would you look like if you believed the things your friends and family thought about you? In reality, trusting someone else's opinion of our character and calling usually looks and sounds far more admirable than our definition. Suddenly, we are free from the burden of self-promotion while leaning into the truth of the deep relationship.

I am now blessed to have these kinds of friends, but this was not always the case. My wife and a few close friends have modelled this so well for me, and the life that comes from these relationships is never-ending. One of my greatest joys is learning this lesson of covenantal friendship; this friendship endures all trials because it is not based on what we need from each other but on what we see will happen through each other if we keep living in honour and love.

Through this laying down, we have all seen a dream come to fruition and continue to unfold. As a group of friends, we are currently watching God unite a city as we have stepped into laying down our lives for the kingdom and one another. I can honestly say that I would not be sitting here writing a book without my amazing wife and some of these close friends. Because of what they have said about me, I have chosen to believe I can achieve such a feat.

For this revelation, I have only God to thank as we prayed these relationships into our lives and serve with them; it is an honour and a privilege.

I feel that this could raise a deep yearning as I type this out. This may be stirring something you haven't known you wanted, or even needed. This could be the desire to find and feel your value. The only way to obtain this is to trust the Father and find people who replicate this culture. If you can't find anyone, become a person like this, and you will attract these kinds of relationships. I need to make clear that this journey of a genuine connection is not one of ease. You will find it hard when you are vulnerable with your newfound friends and family because it will not always look the same as you think it should.

We need to keep in mind on this journey that, first and foremost, you are called to love one another at all costs. After all, Jesus makes it very clear this is how they will know we are different.

People are looking for you to provoke this friendship in their lives. Choking the stronghold of tall poppy in our nation begins with you. I, for one, can't wait to see a generation of celebration instead of competition, applause instead of jealousy, and a united front when it comes to making God famous.

There is one more, deeper, and perhaps more challenging lesson that I have been learning personally that I want to touch on in becoming a friend. We need to address how we express how we are made to feel in our relationships. In my opinion, I am about to make a statement about our emotional state that is and will be one of the most challenging things we ever embark on. In this kind of covenantal relationship, we have no right to make how we feel anybody else's problem. Issues will arise in you, but you need to be responsible for your emotional state.

In my relationship with some friends, I often joked that they possessed the perfect personality type to address the dormant orphan in me. In my experience, through relational breakdown, I would often conclude that they had to be responsible for how they made me feel. But what I have now realised is that I would often confront people on the basis of *what* I was feeling instead of *why* I was feeling it!

I have now learned to find the 'why' behind what I feel before I confront anything with anyone else. This is because I value them and their personal need for a safe relationship. More often than not, my 'why' has nothing to do with them, but they have behaved in a way that sets off a trigger in my life. If we are not careful, we blame the trigger person instead of taking control over the root. Learning this has blessed me with the ability to constantly strengthen my relationship with more complex friendships because I have not burdened them with my emotional state.

This has led me to realise that, in the past, most of the confrontations I have been in have been me trying to scapegoat my need to deal with some stuff that is at the core of my being. If we can find someone to blame for our feelings, we negate our need to master them. In this new model of loving each other, we need to stop giving each other the power over how we feel and instead address the why behind the emotion. This will allow you to reign in the relationship and become a powerful friend.

I encourage you now to take a moment, get out your pen, and write down the dreams of your friends that perhaps you have not championed out of jealousy.

Repent for these moments, set it right, and kill the seed you have been sowing in fear of your pursuit to be something for the kingdom.

Father, we repent now for not championing your children or placing your value over our friends and family. I repent for wanting to be the one that is noticed instead of making you famous. God, you are so gracious and help us become real friends for those around us. Right now, Father, I choose to be a person who champions your children and supports their dreams to come to fruition in you.

THE STORY OF UNDERSTANDING LOVE

My story of understanding love begins with learning about its intention. So often, our level of intimacy is defined by our knowledge and experience of love. To justify how I first knew and understood what I now believe love is, I have to delve into the darker parts of my past when it comes to relationships. The unfortunate truth is that what we think about love defines our view of anything that represents it. This topic has the power to free you to love those around you powerfully and the potential to begin to accept it for yourself. Sounds exciting, doesn't it?

Take a deep breath and dive into vulnerability with me. The way I loved people in my life before this new way of understanding love is not something that I am proud of. My journey in this area is a very personal pain for me.

So, here is my story,

After being saved and having a few years of experience in the church, I met a girl. Without knowing about my brokenness regarding relationships,

I desired deeply to delve right into a romance, not having learned the damage I could cause. This is one of the main reasons we need to be wise and ask ourselves questions concerning our motive before acting on our feelings.

Please don't take this wisdom solely from me but from the book of wisdom itself.

Proverbs 4:23

Keep your heart with all vigilance, for from it flows the springs of life.

Keeping a vigilant heart is so important when dealing with motive. This can be because our feelings can so easily deceive us into thinking we are acting in the desires of God. It is important that we understand when we are making purely emotive decisions. This is not something to be fearful of; simply, it is something that we need to be aware of to monitor the effects it is having on our output relationally, both with others and with God.

Your decisions are consequential and can change the course of others' journeys. My selfish need for love and attention provoked me on a trip I should never have begun. I am glad that the Father uses what is intended for my harm for His good. If this were not the case, I would have felt the shame of my mistakes so deeply that I may never have found the love I have now. Thankfully, we serve a God whose primary concern is leading us into our freedom and not our shame. We see this intent to use the negative for good throughout the foundations of God's character in the book of Genesis.

Genesis 50:20

As for you, you meant evil against me, but God meant it for good, to bring it about that many people should be kept alive, as they are today.

I began to go looking for love in the areas I had always wished to find, and this always took the form of a woman. What happened next was a culmination of my brokenness and the brokenness of the girl whom I had grown to desire deeply. If she were ever to read this (and I hope she does), I would say to her: "It is okay, and I am sorry for the pain I caused. Moreover, I take responsibility for my part in the breakdown in your life and mine." As I explain the context of our relational breakdown, you may find it crazy that I take any form of responsibility for someone else's actions.

What we need to realise is that, when it comes to relationships, if we don't deal with our pain, we place it in the hands of the person we are with as if to say, "Be my saviour, please help me to alleviate this tension in my life." This is often called a scapegoat mechanism in which we shift any sense of responsibility for ourselves onto the actions of others to lessen the feeling of shame in our own lives.

I met this girl at a youth camp where we were both leaders. My best was on display; I had a habit of hiding my mess and not letting people see anything other than what I determined as my profound gifting. In hindsight, this relationship was doomed from the beginning, but we fell into what we thought was love and were both blind to what was about to take place over the next couple of years.

Once this relationship kicked off, I spent weeks in my friend's room agonising because I felt God was saying this was a bad idea. Little did I know that my God would use it to change my view of love completely, and I now understand that I was struggling with what I thought was a bad idea and trying to blame Him for it.

Again, I was looking for a scapegoat to take responsibility for my feelings. Christians often say, "God has told me that my relationship is wrong, and I have to break up with her." If this is something you have done, you need to consider that when you say this to someone, the story they often tell themselves is that God didn't feel they were good enough for you. After a bit of digging, whenever someone has said this, I have found an underlying issue that they don't want to be made to feel responsible for the part of them that is wanting to get out of the relationship. It is far too easy to allow someone to blame God for their decision. This is my story of learning His voice amid that journey.

I fought against the feeling that this relationship was a bad decision and began to convince myself that I was just scared of relationships due to my upbringing. Over time His voice got quieter and quieter, and I could quench these doubts through focusing on pain points in my life instead of how I was feeling. As time went on, I did not realise that I had started to press these doubts onto her as if to say, "Here it is, now can you decide for me." Throughout our relationship, I would keep her in a state of doubt due to my inability to be intimate. She would see my external battle of flesh and spirit as I placed it all on her shoulders to alleviate the agony of uncertainty in my life. It would look like me verbalising all my doubt and fear of love toward her and keeping her in a state of uncertainty while needing her to validate my need to be seen. This was spiritual abuse on my part, as again, I was trying to avoid my responsibility by blaming her and God. I was scapegoating her, and I now believe this was a passive form of emotional abuse in our relationship.

Always trust the unction of His spirit and, in all things, pursue peace beyond understanding. If there is no peace, decide on the facts and not the feelings. If I had listened to my emotional state, perhaps there would have been another way for me to stumble upon this revelation without the immense pain I had to suffer. I do not regret the season for a second, but I will say that if the pain is avoidable, it may be worth it. There are always two ways to learn something, and often we choose the hard way. But please listen to me when I say you don't have to subscribe to learning lessons on your own - you can learn from the mistakes of others.

We had many good times together throughout our relationship and many God times. We would sway back and forward but ultimately were committed to the process of having a relationship - or at least our jaded view of what we thought a relationship was.

Inevitably, after a long time, this dysfunction in our lives led to a mutual dissatisfaction and a secret loathing of one another that we were, (or at least I was) largely unaware of. Due to our needs and insecurity, we stayed in an emotionally abusive relationship until it broke.

At some point, the hiddenness always comes to the surface. I knew it, and she knew it. We weren't happy together, but we refused to make an intelligent decision before it got ugly.

What I thought was love was a vicious cycle of need-based requirements that would and could only be fulfilled in physical acts of love. Use your imagination.

I would get my needs met by having a long theological discussions about me trying to love her and fighting my doubts, these would always end in my fears being eased by a sexual encounter. I would keep her in a state of uncertainty that inevitably would end in her gratifying my need to "feel" that I loved her, and hers was to ensure she felt some kind of love from me.

Unfortunately, I was emotionally abusive, and I had no idea about that. I also had no idea that, due to her upbringing, I may have been perpetuating a cycle that was fulfilling a deficiency of love within her.

It was my genuine desire to love her, but I could not offer her what I had never known or experienced. In reality, all I had to offer was a version of love solely focused on my feelings of satisfaction or dissatisfaction, which could change daily or even hourly.

This led to her cheating on me, where a blame cycle began. So I stood, again playing the victim without looking at my mess. It took quite a while to focus after that, and I now look back on this season with great regret as I understandably misunderstood the situation and began to blame everything except my behaviour.

This break-up was God's grace in my life to find and establish what love indeed was. After a short spiraling into my old habits, I returned to the Father. I spent one of the most potent six months of my faith being shown by His voice how He intended to love me through this season. In this time, some of the most fundamental theologies I hold onto were forged through profound healing encounters surrounding love.

I remember once again coming to the end of my rope. I was sitting on my porch at the top of a three-story building, completely broken and alone, thinking, "Well, it is time to end my life." I said to God that day, "You have five minutes to do something; otherwise, I'll end it." Would you believe it? He did something! At this point, I shouldn't have been surprised at His ability to respond to my idle threats with an immediate response! He called my bluff once again.

My phone rang about three minutes later, and it was my good pal Nathan. Now, this was in 2007. Nathan had just finished his Discipleship Training School with Youth With A Mission and had come back to hear how far I had fallen away. So when I picked up the phone, he invited me to come and share my pain with him.

Everyone needs a Nathan!

Father has a habit of coming through when we need Him. But remember, He is a gentleman, and although He does not require an invitation, He loves one.

This girl was an unwilling participant in my healing journey, and had I walked in a sense of selflessness, she may have been spared some profound journeying. That being said, it is with great faith that I believe if we were ever to converse, she would agree that the Father used this time - not created it but He certainly used it - to grow some deep value in her and me. If I know my Father, and I do, He wastes nothing.

This is where intimacy began for me. But first, I had to understand love. I remember the Father being so available in this season, and one of the things He began to share with me was that the reality that love was not a feeling at all but a choice.

Love is a choice that dictates our feelings, not a feeling that dictates our choices. If you grasp this reality, almost overnight you will go from being a victim in any relationship to being an influential person. You will always, in every situation, have a choice to make.

You see, I had been letting how love 'felt' dictate almost all my behaviours when it came to my relationships with God and others. In fact, every facet of my life was affected by the motive lies surrounding the feeling of love. There is no way that loving based on feeling could have been anything other than self-serving. It was founded on my needs being met instead of meeting a need. Love in and of itself is never meant to be about what you need or want; it is truly a service to another.

Let's look at this biblically and see if we can back it up with great clarity. I believe we can. This is a journey of trust with God, so please don't just take my word for it. Ask Him what He thinks.

In the garden of Gethsemane, we see Jesus in commune with the Father, and what He says should astound us all when it comes to understanding love.

Luke 22:42

Saying, "Father, if you are willing, remove this cup from me. Nevertheless, not my will, but yours, be done."

"If you are willing, remove this cup." Let me paraphrase this: "Father, I don't know if I want to do this!"

The first lesson the Father drew from this period in my life for me was, as I said earlier, that love was a choice and not a feeling. So what we see here is Jesus having a moment of emotion and admitting, "Well, you know what, this looks way too hard, and I don't think I feel like doing it."

When it comes to love, I let my feelings dictate my choices. This is what we all have been taught since the moment we turned on the television. Love was a feeling of intense desire, and it was good – well, at least until we didn't feel it anymore.

The saying goes that you "fall in love." Well, if this is true then you can fall out of it too. There is entirely no commitment involved in a feelings-based love. We get to choose when we are in or out of it, and because we feel like it's over, the other person involved has no say in the matter. With this, there comes no covenant or promise to speak of. For Jesus, there is a far deeper reality at play here regarding love. We see this in his following sentence. He gives us a gift through a more fantastic picture of what love looks like.

"Nevertheless, not my will but yours be done."

What Jesus is saying through this honest and authentic exchange is this: "I'm not feeling it, Father, but because you love these guys so much, I will choose to love, regardless of what I feel." When it came to my relationship, inadvertently, my feelings would lead to getting a need met, but for Jesus, his feelings were secondary to the requirement being fulfilled.

He is the God who meets our needs and offers us his gift of love, and He requires nothing in return.

It can't be about your will and what you want when it comes to love. I have learned that if I meet needs in people's hearts in a healthy way, all mine seem to be completed.

Selfless love; don't let your feelings dictate your choices. If you choose to believe that God loves you, let that be the foundation of your decisions in your life. Do not act on how you feel when you are lacking in confidence in His love toward you. Stand firm in the truth that he has chosen you because He wants to not because He felt like it.

This reality, for me, has led to intimacy on far deeper levels, and it was all because I responded to the depth of God's call from the midst of my pain.

One of the best places and examples of how God loves us is through the consistent decision Jesus makes in His life to restore even those who haven't asked Him. Such as at the wedding of Cana, where the character of God was put on display in the form of a miracle.

Perhaps we should start this thought with the beginning of Jesus' public ministry at the ripe old age of thirty. We see Jesus paint a prophetic picture of what is to come through his life in this story. The gospel is not only a story of salvation but also an invitation to return to what it was we were designed for.

I will tackle this thought in depth through the last chapter of this book. It was a more profound action than simple salvation from our rebellion and a call to return to belonging. This will change everything for you regarding your interaction with love. After all, He is love, and this is His definition of himself. So, it stands to reason that if we are experiencing a false version of His love through the lenses of religious control, or even a simple misunderstanding, then we will incorporate this into our lives and reflect it into all the experiences of the flesh we have regarding love.

He is inviting you into restoration.

It is interesting to me that Jesus, in the first public display of His glory, was at a wedding. We have all read the story countless times before, and unfortunately, it has mostly been talked about and shared as backing that God isn't against drinking alcohol. But here, we find a far more profound reality.

First, we have to ask ourselves a few questions: why was Jesus' mother so interested in the fact that the hosts were running out of wine?

John 2:3

When the wine ran out, the mother of Jesus said to him, "They have no wine."

I love this scripture for a few reasons. First, here we get to see the divine hand of God being motivated by human emotion, but why? Jesus' mother was worried and for a good reason. We have no idea if she is somehow connected to this family, but she takes it upon herself to have God intervene. In the Jewish culture, there is what I would call a social law in place when it comes to weddings: if you were to run out of wine, you would be shamed and deemed an outcast from society. In light of this, we see the mother of Jesus concerning herself with the social standing of this family and asking Jesus to do something to help them.

At its very core, the foundation of this miracle was the restorative relational nature of God being put on display. The religious have focused on the behavioural aspect, asking, "Did Jesus drink the wine, or worse, condone drinking?" Yet, God looks past the behavioural factor and directly into the current need for protection and restoration, looking at loving people for nothing in return.

John 2:4

And Jesus said to her, "Woman, what does this have to do with me? My hour has not yet come."

I find it interesting that Jesus made the statement, "My time has not yet come." Yet, with little argument, He submitted to the need His mother saw and performed His first awe-inspiring miracle.

He made a prophetic statement here:

"I have not come to judge your actions, but instead, I have come to ensure you are not ashamed, and I will turn this water into wine so that you can see me for who I am."

God's heart is drawn to those cast out in society, and here He takes the opportunity to prevent shame in one family's life.

John 2:7

Jesus said to the servants, "Fill the jars with water." And they filled them up to the brim.

John 2:9

When the master of the feast tasted the water now become wine and did not know where it came from (though the servants who had drawn the water knew), the master of the feast called the bridegroom.

Here is the crux of this story; Jesus's actions extended past salvation and into restoration, but now we see a divine repositioning in society.

John 2:10

And said to him, "Everyone serves the good wine first, and when people have drunk freely, then the poor wine. But you have kept the good wine until now."

It would stand to reason that if shame was the cost of running out of wine, then saving even better wine until last would have socially put them in higher regard.

This is love. I would say that Jesus' response to His mother revealed that He wasn't looking for an opportunity for a big miracle. When He was presented with a significant need before Him, compassion caused His heart to partner with His mothers yearning to see a social salvation. This caused Jesus to jump in and save the day. This is an excellent example of the restorative nature that Jesus displays throughout His ministry time on earth. He will not only desire to save you, but also to elevate you beyond your situation and into something new, something beautiful, something packed full of mystery and self-acceptance.

Another example we can also look at would be how Jesus picked people to follow Him who needed restoration. The disciples were all fishermen and carpenters. Within the context of the Jewish religious system in Galilee, to become anything less than a disciple was considered a social failure. So, when the words were uttered to the emerging disciples of Jesus, "Come follow me," it was a re-establishment of their position in culture. These men and women that were chosen throughout the ministry of the rabbi Jesus were experiencing a social reformation of status. After being rejected by the system, they are given not only a second chance but also an opportunity to learn at the feet of God.

God loves this action; He loves to restore you through your failures. Therefore, I am giving you my failures as a catalyst for His glory. I know that if you can change your view of the purpose of failure in your life, you will see He has chosen you like the disciples because once you find the power in His nature of restoration you will carry the revelation to free others from their shame.

The need we have to truly understand love toward ourselves is what will set you free to love others well. I have had to go through pain to learn that I misunderstood Him. Unfortunately, on my journey to realise that I had dysfunction, there was a cost of wounding others, and this is where grace needs to be applied.

Your story of love may look very different from mine. Still, I know this; if we can sit and genuinely ask, "How am I giving love and how am I receiving it?" then I can guarantee that some relationships you are in right now would benefit from this kind of self-discovery.

How I viewed love in this relationship was shattered by the reality that I believed God had to love me, but I didn't necessarily think that He wanted to. Of course, this all stemmed from the belief that I was not loveable in the first place. So a part of my relational breakdown was based on my need to self-sabotage so I could again blame someone for this happening in my life.

When the relationship finally broke down, and she cheated on me, I have to say that God was making it apparent to me that I had brought this on myself. I needed to take responsibility for some of her actions. This broke something in me, and suddenly, I began to take responsibility, and freedom began to come.

I wonder how many of us spend our time asking God why He isn't moving in the areas we need Him instead of sitting and asking Him what He needs in relationship with us?

For me, up until this revelation of choice-based love, my prayer life was filled with need-based requests and no relational discourse. Now, I have the immense pleasure of walking with God in a constant state of conversation, which leads me deeper into His heart, and I will be forever grateful.

Jesus chose to love the family involved at the wedding. He didn't have to, He had no moral obligation to, but he wanted to. This is how I believe he feels about you and I. God didn't have to clothe us in the garden and send Jesus to win us back! He wanted to. You were His desire, and you still are.

Father, help us to receive your love. More than this, Lord, help us walk in conversation with you with prayers of connection instead of requirements needing to be met. Help us, Father, be known by you and know you. You have been so kind to me in my life, and for that, you can have it all.

Adam Thurling

The Journey

THE STORY OF TENSION BETWEEN GRACE AND TRUTH

As I grew in my faith, I became more and more confused. The God I met in the park, and the one I was presented with in the church, were not matching up. I had two realities taught to me in the early stages of my faith. Number one, I was made in God's image and that I was somehow worth something to this king, and number two, I was a sinner, a mess and if I was able to admit that before Him I would be saved by grace. Now, I don't currently subscribe to the label of a sinner as my identity - you may have already picked this up.

On the journey toward this shift aways from that label, there were many lessons that I had to sift through to change how I viewed myself. However, even for those who have not yet engaged in these kinds of relational conversations with God, there may be a truth here that will set you on a crash course with honest dialogue and a radical encounter around the personal view you carry of yourself.

So here we go; this is a massive topic!

To continue holding the view that you are but a filthy rag that God has graciously valued, even after God Himself, has taken on the title of a sinner for you, is simply a lie! This lie seems to somehow speak to our inability to see ourselves as of any value to God. We adhere to it because it makes us comfortable in the self-loathing belief systems that keep us from our calling. There is no risk in believing in a God with no relational requirements. This is why we see people still trapped in the old covenant mentality of appeasing a God who, above anything else, is angry at sin in my life. "If I can just live up to these standards, I will be able to live in peace believing that I am okay with God." This mentality is the basis of religion. This is the very thing I feel called to crush in the lives around me. This is also the foundation of performance ministry. It's the profound inability to be vulnerable and transparent with God while we present a depth founded on our fear of exposure instead of our security in intimacy.

You, my friends, are so worth the love He has lavished on you, and there is more you can have. When we believe in the relational paradigm with God, we realise that it is not our behaviour that qualifies us; it is our intimacy. Our relational equity with God empowers us to live in and from the culture of heaven. This is not a grace that will empower you to sin. When it is taught well it will provoke a lifestyle of response to love that will inevitably produce deep desire righteousness in you to become like Christ. This is the only way a lifestyle of righteousness can be sustainable, as its strength isn't in you but the love He has for you.

2 Corinthians 5:14-15

For the love of Christ controls us because we have concluded this: that one has died for all; therefore, all have died; and he died for all, that those who live might no longer live for themselves but for him who for their sake died and was raised.

The more we love, the more we become like Him, and as we fall deeper in love, we start to change the realities in which we live. This will inevitably happen as he reveals deeply who He truly is to us. This thought could radically change everything for you. What if the foundation of your struggle was simply the inability to believe that even in your mess, you are of intrinsic value to God?

One thing that I cannot get past in the prodigal story is that the son who left with his inheritance in hand never moved away from the reality that he always remained a son. He knew that at any moment, he could turn back from his wicked ways and step into an embrace.

This picture of the prodigal living as a sinner, who had always remained a son, perplexed me. This couldn't be true, could it? I thought that my sin hindered my connection with God, and He surely couldn't love me until I repented. This is where the tension between grace and truth begins. The reality is that sin caused distance between God and me, yet He died for it not to have that kind of power. Perhaps there is powerful freedom in the idea that God is not offended by sin but walks with us towards freedom.

In this chapter, I want to take you on the journey of discovery that I went through in scripture to understand precisely what we should believe about the consequence of sin and disbelief. So strap yourself in as I make numerous statements in the following pages of this book. I hope that I have laid the necessary foundations for you to trust my heart in what I am about to express, and remember that this is a book about a journey and not about absolutes!

I am about to explore the depth of sonship that God has called us into while disputing the focus on our sin and, worse, the sins we believe we see in each other.

The scriptures say that Jesus died for the sins of the world, not just for those who believe but also for those who don't. So one thing we have done in our fallen state is carry a behavioural definition of sin. This is not locked up in the New Testament reality of love, we have carried over the definition of sin given to us in the old covenant teaching of self-atonement through sacrifice.

1 John 2:2

He is the propitiation for our sins, and not for ours only but also the sins of the whole world.

We have done a great disservice to the gospel by teaching that its focus is on our freedom from sin. We have accepted Jesus as our Saviour, and this has defeated our separation from Him, but this is just the beginning. It is true that the beginning of our journey starts with belief in this salvation, but this is not the whole picture.

We are free because he has restored us to a right relationship through a once-and-for-all sacrifice that has completed the law, and that sacrifice stands in our lives whether we believe it or not! I hear the gasps out loud, hear me out. Sin has been atoned for in the world, It is within our relationships with God that we find our freedom. Now, we know that this does not give us a license to go out and have a great time in the town and have the audacity to believe we are in a good place on our journey. The reality is that if we genuinely accept grace, then there is some kind of fruit to testify to that. When you become a son and move away from your sin, the truth is that it does not look like freedom to sin but instead freedom from sin.

Truly fruitful repentance is implemented into our lives through an all-empowering love that makes you ask the continual question, "Father, is this pleasing to you?" But when you are focused on a behavioural response of repentance, your conversation always begins with a statement of self-loathing; "I am not worthy of your love. Could you please forgive me?" Therefore, I would like to suggest that our repentance, in the model of love, should sound more like an awareness of missing an opportunity to represent him correctly in our lives. We have spent far too many years offering God an apology for being a dirty, filthy sinner unworthy of His love, while He waited patiently for us to accept His kindness.

With this reality of freedom from sin, there comes a responsibility to be an example of the Father on earth. The more you love Him, the less you desire the things that damage your relationship with Him. Think of it like this: I love my wife with everything I have, so I continually decide not to damage that relationship with things that will hurt her. It is the same with God. The emphasis should have never been placed on your behaviour but on your response to love. This repentance is a relational model. It should sound like this, "I am deeply in love with God, and this is not pleasing to Him, so I will not partake in it." It was never about your behaviour but entirely about your response.

We need to understand that there are two different identities we can live from in these two realities. We either live in 'sinnership' or 'sonship,' and both manifest other realities when communicating with the Father.

I stand firm on our identity as sons regardless of our position in belief. That being said, I still maintain that if you don't believe and don't have faith in the love of the Father, there is a consequence in our choice, instead of a punishment from God. When sharing these thoughts, I often get asked, "Well, why does God punish sin?" We need to realise that the result of sin is birthed in our decision to choose it over love. My Father does not send people to hell, He also does not force them to accept him!

At His core, He is a gentleman. The consequence of hell is found in the reality of our choice. Despite all He has done, we choose to neglect a love that has cost us nothing, and that choice lands us in hot water. God does not send people to hell, We simply choose it. His offer is freedom in relationships, and the benefits are a lifestyle founded on that freedom.

This is the classic scapegoat mentality; "God will punish me for my behaviour; therefore, He is not loving." My reality is this; it is not so much a consequence of sin as a consequence of not partaking in a relationship. I also believe that this is a consequence of our own free will and not God perpetrating violence on disobedience.

We don't need to look beyond the person of Christ described in Hebrews one verse three to understand how the Father feels about sin; *"He is the radiance of the glory of God and the exact imprint of his nature, and he upholds the universe by the word of his power. After making purification for sins, he sat down at the right hand of the Majesty on high."*

We see throughout the New Testament that Jesus, in His wisdom, allowed people to abandon themselves to their own choices, and He did this without His judgment attached to their actions. Yet, when we live in a sinful state, in reality, we judge ourselves as unlovable and unacceptable. This is the same belief the prodigal had as he walked up to his driveway as he returned home.

He rehearsed his inability to believe he was acceptable to his father based on his actions; "Father, I have sinned against you; let me just be a servant in your house." He did not believe his father would love him enough to restore him to his original position of sonship.

This sounds vaguely familiar to the actions of Adam hiding in the garden. Let me tell you, getting free from this thinking will break you into freedom from the behaviours you hate. You go from a struggle to quitting watching porn, drinking, or sleeping around to becoming completely and utterly captured by love.

Once you understand the nature of love, you will be changed forever. The Father's response will challenge anyone with a performance relationship with God, desiring to be accepted based on their excellent behaviour. The son reaches his father in the prodigal story and makes his plea! What do we see the father do? He simply ignores his son's repentance, calls for the restorative ring and a robe, and celebrates his decision to come home.

This reality and freedom were not always the case in my life. Let me tell you a story of a boy angry and confused with God! Sound familiar?

As you have read in previous chapters, I met our Father in a park in the middle of my darkest hour.

On that day, there was no prerequisite for my encounter. It was pure and unrestrained love based on His desire to know me and for me to know Him.

The journey that ensued afterwards was one of learning and receiving his love, and what I was learning was that there was this thing they called grace and this thing they called sin. Unfortunately, it didn't all add up for me over the coming years. Evil seemed to find its foothold in my shame for participating in things that were deemed unacceptable in God's sight. I believed God only applied grace in my repentance. It seemed I had to feel shame before I could feel love, which caused a deep dysfunction in my relationship with God. I was so confused, when I met love in that park, He required nothing of me; there was no repentance, just a radical feeling of acceptance.

I have said it before; I subconsciously believed He was my God and my abuser. Although I was unaware of it, this was my reality. I treated God with a deep mistrust due to my misunderstanding. This misunderstanding was founded on the tension in meeting a God that extended me free grace and the reality that I was taught that in dealing with my sin I had to change to become more like Him.

Because of this tension in myself there was one question that seemed always to leave me deflated, "If God is so good then why is there so much evil in the world?"

Here is the thing. Lying dormant in our subconscious - and for some of us, our conscious – is the same niggling question that the devil planted in Eve's ear at the very conception of sin; "Is God perfect? Did God say?"

It's taken around ten years for me to find answers around all of this, and I am still working on it. I have been both a mess and a message in this time of walking out relational trust with God. How could God be both a God of grace and consequence, and how could I preach the gospel and go straight back into the distress patterns as soon as I entered the safety of my own home? It didn't add up. I couldn't trust His character because He seemed to be bipolar at best.

First, let's tackle how I could be leading people to Christ, operating in anointing and setting captives free, whilst at the same time being a drunken mess, a compulsive liar, and worse.

I was undergoing a process. Let's take a look.

Our nature is simultaneously righteous and sinful. Nevertheless, our spiritual reality is what we know Christ has achieved for us through His sacrifice. Understanding this is important and can change how we respond to the Father amid our fallen state. This, at its core, is about what we believe the Father believes about us.

This can produce either an unmeasurable steadfastness in Him, or on the flip side it can produce an apathetic approach to living in an honourable way through Him. We struggle in this life to choose righteousness in a way that would promote Godliness to the world. Are we waiting for a revelation, or is it our responsibility to make the change? I believe we have used God's grace as a scapegoat for our actions for far too long, but there is truth in this reality that the Father's love is everlasting. We will soon explore this through Hebrews in conjunction with the other side of this reality but for now, let's carry on.

We must begin with our current truth, so let's establish that first! What do we know that the Father says about us through the sacrifice of Christ?

In John 1:12 (We are children of God), Colossians 2:9-10 (We have been brought to fullness), 1 Cor 6:17 (we are with him in one spirit), Romans 6:6 (crucified with him so our body ruled by sin might be done away with). When we abide in Christ, we have a new reality, and it's the reality that the Father no longer sees us in a defective state. Paul calls this a new creation.

It says in 1 John 3:5-8

You know that he appeared to take away sins, and there is no sin in him. No one who abides in him keeps on sinning; no one who keeps on sinning has either seen him or known him.

No one who abides in him keeps on sinning? This is where we need to define what abiding is. If you just read over that scripture, you would read it within a behavioural context. Abiding must mean doing the things that keep us in a relationship, right?

The literal meaning of this word is to remain or to stay with. It is used in both a literal sense and a metaphorical sense. To me, abiding seems to give the connotation of staying the course, enduring to the end, and ultimately choosing to walk with and believe Christ no matter what you think or feel about yourself; just trust Him.

When we abide in Christ, as I mentioned earlier, we lose our desire to sin because when we stay with Him, we choose not to allow our shame to dictate the terms of our relationship but instead trust Christ in what He has said He achieved for us. This helps us fall deeply in love with Him, which stops the sin cycle.

As I just mentioned, we also know that we have a sin default by our significantly fallen nature, and we get stuck in living with the reality of this. Wouldn't it be helpful if we could grasp some understanding of this reality?

It continues in 1 John 3:7-8

Little children, let no one deceive you.
Whoever practices righteousness is righteous,
as he is righteous. Whoever makes a practice
of sinning is of the devil, for the devil has been
sinning from the beginning.

Anyone who "practices righteousness": this is active participation in what Jesus has achieved for us, for none are righteous, not even one, unless through the blood of the lamb. We practice righteousness, or our right standing, in the same way; we abide in truth through trust that Jesus is whom He says He is and has achieved what He says that he has. I know I am repeating myself here, but we need to learn this to be set free. There is something more important at stake here: we need this to better present the true living God's love for them, not based on condition but a wilful desire to go to the cross to know Him and be known by Him.

Romans 3:21-24

But now, the righteousness of God has been
manifested apart from the law, although the
Law and the Prophets bear witness to it - the
righteousness of God through faith in Jesus
Christ for all who believe. For there is no
distinction: for all have sinned and fell short
of the glory of God, and are justified by his
grace as a gift, through the redemption that is
in Christ Jesus.

Being sons, we cannot dispute that our spiritual state is righteousness. But how do we walk this out in a flesh state where sin is still rife? God became flesh, so who is there better to learn from than Him in how to live in a way that represents God to the world. He struggled with the same struggles we do so that He could atone for them on the cross.

We know that Christ was fully human.

Philippians 2:6-8

Who, though he was in the form of God, did not count equality with God a thing to be grasped but emptied himself by taking the form of a servant, being born in the likeness of men. And being found in human form, he humbled himself by becoming obedient to the point of death, even death on a cross.

And we know that He is entirely God.

Matt 1:23

"Behold, the virgin shall conceive and bear a son, and they shall call his name Immanuel" (Which means God with us).

Would it be wrong of us to consider then that Christ, who lived with the spiritual reality of being the Son of God, had to will his flesh into submission to His spiritual truth instead of building His truth on what His flesh was experiencing? Our spiritual reality is that we are made complete in Christ to make this clearer. Often though, as has been the case in my life, what we feel is true dictates the terms of our reality.

Therefore, we should be transforming our flesh reality into submission to what is confirmed through the spirit. The best example of this is in the garden of Gethsemane.

Luke 22:41

Saying, "Father, if you are willing, remove this cup from me. Nevertheless, not my will, but yours, be done." And there appeared to him an angel from heaven, strengthening him.

As we touched on earlier, here, Jesus in His 'humanity' looks to be asking for a way out of the task set before Him. He had to have his flesh reality reminded by the spiritual truth As a son of God he had to submit to the truth that this was His calling despite how He was feeling.

In my own experience, it is much the same for us. It cannot be disputed that we are called to be sons on the earth. In the words of Jesus, "They will do greater things than me." But unfortunately, we are a generation of children who are irrefutably not willing to take our part in living this out. We are too busy trying to figure out whether God is actually for us. I have had many conversations about this with people, and it always lands in the same place: they are waiting for God to change them. After all, he is in control - right?

Like Christ, we need to partner with our spiritual reality and will our flesh into submission to our spiritual existence!

1 John 3:8

The reason the Son of God appeared was to destroy the devil's works.

He didn't come to make us drones without free will. We chose the first tree, and now we need to select the second. Jesus is that second tree. Will we choose life and life abundant, or knowledge of good and evil again?

The difference between our case and that of Adam and Eve, is that in the garden there was no sin consciousness. But does that mean the desires weren't there? Maybe it simply implies that the motivation was not to seek love outside God's embrace.

Paul sums this up for the church of Corinth.

1 Cor.5:1-11

For we know that if the tent, our earthly home, is destroyed, we have a building from God, a house not made with hands, eternal in the heavens. For in this tent, we groan, longing to put on our heavenly dwelling if, indeed by putting it on, we may not be found naked. For a while, we are still in this tent; we groan, being burdened - not that we would be unclothed, but that we would be further clothed so that what is mortal may be swallowed up by life. He who has prepared us for this very thing is God, who has given us the Spirit as a guarantee. So we are always of good courage. We know that while we are at home in the body, we are away from the Lord, for we walk by faith, not by sight. Yes, we are of good courage, and we would rather be away from the body and at home with the Lord. So whether we are at home or away, we make it our aim to please him, for we must all appear before the judgment seat of Christ so that each one may receive what is due for what he has done in the body, whether good or evil.

Therefore, knowing the fear of the Lord, we persuade others. But God knows what we are, and I hope it is also known to your conscience.

Yes, we are responsible for our conscience, for this surely would be the fruit of eating the tree of the knowledge of good and evil. Once we ate of the tree, we took responsibility for having that experience. Before the fall, I am not confident we would have needed a conscience.

Perhaps we should end this thought with Paul's words to his disciple Timothy.

1 Timothy 4:7

Have nothing to do with irreverent, silly myths. Instead, train yourself for godliness.

The irreverent myth here is: "God is in control and responsible for changing you." You, friends, need to choose to become like Him and work at it. There is no magic remedy for your struggle except that you can engage with the cross that has set you free and will change your life. So today, employ your will and become like Him. You won't win the battle with your struggle by fighting it. Instead, you will have a victory through falling in love with the grace that entangles you through our loving and astounding God, Jesus Christ of Nazareth.

We know that He does not control what we become, so what is the foundation of significant change within us?

There needs to be a pivotal realisation of what provokes us to eradicate 'sin' in our lives. Remember, above all else it is the love of Christ that controls us.

The only way to sustainably change our behavioural course is to know our value in the midst of it, "For the love of Christ controls us."

When we have a realisation of pure love, we respond to it. It compels us or controls us to change, not because it makes us take action, but its very nature helps us desire to please it.

Here is a new reality for us all to live by.

Grace is offered in and through the sanctification process, and that process looks like journeying through the change in response to love. However, there is still a consequence to sin. As we see in the fall story, every action has its reaction. I believe this is where we hold the tension between grace and truth.

2 Corinthians 7:10

Godly grief produces a repentance that leads to salvation without regret, whereas worldly grief produces death.

2 Corinthians 7:11

For see what earnestness this godly grief has produced in you, but also what eagerness to clear yourselves, what indignation, what fear, what longing, what zeal, what punishment! At every point, you have proved yourselves innocent in the matter.

But without this godly grief, amid the abuse of grace, we see the reality of how we respond to love. If we stay the course and go on the journey of love, the process will look messy but has a redemptive purpose. But, on the other hand, we get lost if we see this love as a permission point for our brokenness without a desire to change.

Hebrews 10:3

But in these sacrifices, there is a reminder of sins every year.

Throughout the Old Testament, the sacrifices remained as a reminder of sin. They were still a cleansing point but necessary for our conscience to grasp holiness. Jesus now serves as this reminder of the cost of corruption: its wages are death, and He paid its price.

One of the most convincing statements by the author of Hebrews when responding to the knowledge of pure love in holiness is found in chapter 10.

Hebrews 10:5-12

Consequently, when Christ came into the world, he said,

"Sacrifices and offerings you have not desired, but a body have you prepared for me;

in burnt offerings and sin offerings

you have taken no pleasure.

Then I said, 'Behold, I have come to do your will, O God,

as it is written of me in the scroll of the book.'"

When he said above, "You have neither desired nor taken pleasure in sacrifices and offerings and burnt offerings and sin offerings" (these are offered according to the law), then he added, <u>"Behold, I have come to do your will" He does away with the first to establish the second. And by that will, we have been sanctified through the offering of the body of Jesus Christ once for all.</u>

*And every priest stands daily at his service,
offering repeatedly the same sacrifices, which
can never take away sins. But when Christ had
offered for all time a single sacrifice for sins,
he sat down at the right hand of God.*

We can't get past it; there are some severe consequences. How do we reconcile this with the understanding of the nature of God being love? We need to be reminded that we make the choices that cause the consequences. God does not punish sin; otherwise, Jesus went through severe agony for nothing. This means that we choose Heaven or hell - He does not send anyone there. For His desire and will is that all should be saved.

Hebrews 10:26

*If we go on sinning deliberately after receiving
the knowledge of the truth, there no longer
remains a sacrifice for sins.*

Hebrews 10:27

*But a fearful expectation of judgment and a
fury of fire that will consume the adversaries.*

This is why I believe Paul clarifies that we should not go on sinning after receiving grace!

Romans 6:1-6

*What shall we say then? Are we to continue in
sin that grace may abound? By no means! How
can we who died to sin still live in it? Do you
not know that all of us who have been baptised
into Christ Jesus were baptised into his death?*

We were buried, therefore, with him by baptism into death so that, just as Christ was raised from the dead by the glory of the Father, we too might walk in the newness of life.

If we have been united with him in a death like his, we shall undoubtedly be connected in a resurrection like his. We know that our old self was crucified with him so that the body of sin might be brought to nothing so that we would no longer be enslaved to sin.

Here is the question I am left asking; "What then are we to do with the Law of Moses?" Statements come to mind from all those who use the sacrifice of Jesus as a reason to sin instead of freedom from sin; "Don't be so religious." The reality is this; the Law of Moses is good for us, and in conjunction with love, living out these "laws" actually looks like living as a good person.

You shall have no other gods before me.

You shall not make for yourself an idol in the form of anything.

You shall not misuse the name of the Lord your God.

Remember the Sabbath day by keeping it holy.

Honour your Father and your mother.

You shall not murder.

You shall not commit adultery.

You shall not steal.

You shall not give false testimony against your neighbour.

You shall not covet your neighbour's house, wife, or property.

None of these laws are inherently unfair or designed to stop us from having a good life. On the contrary, these laws are designed to help us reign in this world. Why do we react to these things regarding religious spirits? It is solely due to our inability to see the heart of God through instruction. Through Christ, we are given freedom through the process of sanctification, not permission to abandon sense in living out holiness.

Hebrews 10:28

Anyone who has set aside the Law of Moses dies without mercy on the evidence of two or three witnesses.

Father's design for us is that we work this out in the process and enjoy the learning. We all know the scripture,

"*Therefore, my beloved, as you have always obeyed, so now, not only as in my presence but much more in my absence, work out your salvation with fear and trembling*" *(Philippians 2:12)*

This is better translated as: "Work out your salvation in awe and wonder." Fear implies that we are to do this because God will be mad if we don't.

I don't agree with this to being the case; we work it out because it is a process of awe and adoration of what He has done for us.

It is our responsibility to do this, and His love provokes us, but as soon as we start to excuse our behaviour through grace, we have missed the point of grace altogether. So take the journey of sanctification, and don't sear your conscience in the name of what you would deem to be freed because it feeds your flesh. You are called to be free from sin, not free to sin, and this is the fruit of knowing you are loved and living in Christ. You are not loved because you behave, but you will end up behaving because you are loved.

Galatians 5:1

For freedom, Christ has set us free; stand firm, therefore, and do not submit again to a yoke of slavery.

1 Corinthians 6:12

"All things are lawful for me," but not all things are helpful. "All things are lawful for me," but I will not be dominated by anything.

Galatians 5:13 - 14

For you were called to freedom, brothers. Only do not use your freedom as an opportunity for the flesh, but through love, serve one another. The whole law is fulfilled in one word: "You shall love your neighbour as yourself."

We must be careful not to lose this reality of response to love in our generation. It is all too tempting to neglect and forget the cost that Jesus paid and water it down in our desperate attempt to feel accepted and loved in this world. When we are firmly wrapped up in the love of Christ, we don't desire these things. And why would we? They don't sound all that appealing when you measure them up to the pleasure of the Father.

The tension to hold on this topic is that encountering love is the turning point; we can't do it through works, only through faith empowered by love.

I challenge you in this space, where we struggle to let go of our performance, just to lie down and invite Him into being known by you. Prepare your heart before entering the next chapter, as it may be a tough one to swallow.

I wanted to use scripture in this chapter to speak for itself. Fortunately, I am not foolish enough to believe that I alone have the wisdom to express what has changed my life so profoundly towards Him.

We need to understand the word of God rightly, so here I want to place the same disclaimer I set at the beginning of this book: this is my current position on all these thoughts, and it is my journey I am inviting you to partner with. I want to encourage you to form opinions on these topics and take them to God to assess and address correctly for your journey. You will have different questions to ask the Father and various issues to address with Him. I encourage you to not just merely read this and be convinced but to step into your reality with Him on this journey into His heart.

Adam Thurling

The Journey

THE STORY OF THE GOSPEL

It was a relatively normal day at work. At this stage in my life, I worked as a gym sales representative. Due to my nature and care for people and their general well-being (mental and otherwise), this job was perfect for me in this season. I had started walking in the realities of what we have explored together throughout this book around God's character. My views had changed drastically about His character and love, and I was about to have an encounter with a young man who was going to show me the fruit of these realities. I had begun to believe that God was good and only had my best in mind, laying to rest the model of self-loathing faith I had been taught on a subconscious level.

We have to understand that, in the gospel of Jesus, we have something far more profound than a mere salvation story alone. In it, we find answers to the age-old question; "Am I lovable? What am I worth, and how do I find the purpose to my life in a world that seems to devalue my very being in every sense?"

In this, the last part of our journey together within the pages of this book, I intend to present a simple truth that lies in plain sight within the gospel. I believe that if I had realised this in the early stages of my faith, it would have transformed the way I expressed God to others. This perhaps, would have had a far more profound impact on the lives of those around me. It is a reality that will help you drop your desire for judgment and justice. My prayer is that it will transform you into loving like Jesus. We are called to look like love to the world, and Jesus is the example of how to walk that out. So, as we delve deeper into loving Jesus, we are transformed into His likeness, and perhaps more profoundly, we become His mouthpiece for forgiveness and restoration in the world.

John 10-23

Jesus said to them again, "Peace be with you. As the Father has sent me, even so, I am sending you." And when he had said this, he breathed on them and said to them, "Receive the Holy Spirit. If you forgive the sins of any, they are forgiven; if you withhold forgiveness from any, it is withheld."

The prayer that I have begun to pray in my life does not cry out for help to be changed, but instead one in which I pray to understand who He is and how He loves me deeply. This helps me to become empowered to change through the reality of being loved. This replaces my need to believe I am inherently evil. It kills my need to feel guilt and lessens the weight that my shame has in demishinshing my ability to receive love; I will say this a few times throughout this chapter: Jesus' mission was not one where we need to believe to belong, but instead, His invitation is to belong; so that He can journey with us toward believing.

Are you ready for another story? Please take a deep breath, and let's enjoy this one!

When I worked as a gym sales representative on this seemingly ordinary day, a young man walked up to my desk. As he was approaching me, I noticed a gentleman who seemed to carry a deep kindness amid some genuine and evident pain. Yet, through his demeanour, I could tell without discernment - or any spiritual gift - that he was tired, lonely, and had been beaten up by the brutality that we have to face on a day-to-day basis in our world.

He began to explain to me that he had a need to feel better about himself and wanted to make, in his own words, "Some better decisions" in life, and that started with joining a gym. The most interesting part of this is that he would, throughout our conversation, begin to tell me over and over how he didn't want to feel pressured to join up, and he was here to have a look at our facility.

Deep compassion grew inside me while he talked to me about his lifestyle and current situation. I quickly swayed the conversation away from what he needed to change about himself to how I could help him. I asked him if I could give him advice, to which he promptly replied, "Yes."

Let me start by sharing that I didn't say, bro, all you need is Jesus. Before I carried the understanding of this refreshing evangelism style that I tend to walk in now, my advice would have sounded something like that. Although accurate, I understand that this response is entirely unhelpful to someone whose primary issue is believing they are of any value to anyone.

It is essential to understand that this statement is not advice, although it is true that Jesus is the answer to the issues we face in this world. Simply making that statement is unhelpful and, frankly, a little dismissive of the humanity that stands before us. It is also a statement that can heap on the shame of helplessness and perpetuate a victim-based faith. We know a Jesus who will help someone through their issues in life, but He will not allow them to use Him as a crutch for too long without empowering them to take responsibility and make changes.

This can only occur if we offer the tools needed to mature into a place of self-awareness. But, again, this all begins with not playing the blame game and taking responsibility for our stuff.

When we present the gospel as a medication for the pains of this life, we cheapen the power in the journey with Him through it. The good news is that there is a love that will sustain you through it all, but it is essential to realise that true love will begin to transform you through a series of deep and meaningful conversations surrounding the issues in your heart that are preventing your freedom.

Now, let me just say I do not negate that there are people who have had, and will have, experiences of miraculous and instantaneous deliverance from the stuff in their lives. Still, by and large, we have a generation of people who cling to the hope of this happening while staying in their mess! We need to be sure that we empower these people to walk in the art of genuine and honest dialogue with the Father and process it out to see the fruit of love become real in their lives.

People need to see why they need Jesus in their life, for most of us His love has to collide with our inability to love ourselves.

This old style of presenting the gospel speaks to a desire in us to shirk off our responsibility in journeying with the person in front of us. You see, we have made a grave mistake in evangelism if we believe God's intention is simply fulfilled in a moment of accepting Jesus. We are the victims of an old-school mentality that heaped shame on the Christian for not getting people saved traditionally. This young man needed an invitation to a conversation about why God could help him and how much he was loved.

My advice, in this instance, sounded something like this:

"Mate, because I care about you and want to see you succeed, can I share my weight loss story with you?"

(Wait, you didn't preach to him?)

Of all things, I began to explain how I had experienced a liver cleanse that was the catalyst for me to lose some weight. We had a great conversation through this, which helped this young man feel understood and seen. My intention was not to talk about Jesus at all. I wanted to restore this guy in being seen for who he was and not for being a prize to add to my salvation tally. At best, we are naïve and sometimes intentionally ignorant, if we think people cannot detect our underlying motive in caring for them. We can love and care for someone in order to get them saved, or, we can love like Jesus would have despite what they end up believing. In my experience this old method of evangelism only really shows People that they are worth loving or helping if they believe the same things as I do. This second way that I am presenting is a pure love that will be sustained by peoples active free choice to accept it.

We love to be correct, and we love to help, but we need to try not to love out of a motive to feel of some value to someone's life or for any other selfish motive. Instead, we love because their life depends on unlocking their ability to accept the loving nature of God. As Christians, we need to live out this kind of love whether they end up believing in Him or not. It is not a 'love if they believe' model that Jesus has told us to follow. Unfortunately, somehow that is what we have presented to the world, and let me tell you, they are holding us accountable for this double standard.

How on earth do we fix this? Let's get back to the story.

I had to decide, at this point, to either take the age-old route of telling someone how much they needed Jesus because of what they had done wrong in their life. But in this instance I decided to partner with the new nature of Jesus that had been revealed to me and begin to restore this young man's view of himself through the lense of a truly all loving and accepting God.

I was looking at a guy who already knew his shortcomings. He was already depressed, hurt and anxious, and for all I knew, most of his life was riddled with the mentality that being accepted meant he needed to change because something was wrong with him.

One of our most significant failings as believers is the presentation of a gospel that only allows you to belong when you believe.

Currently, the way we present the 'good news' in this model sounds something like this. "If you admit all your faults and come to a realisation of your deep shame, then repent and pray for God to enter your heart, He will accept you, even as filthy as you are, but only once you have admitted that you are a worthless piece of trash without Him." I would like to suggest that this is abusive and unhelpful in our expression of who God is to us, and it can take years to undo the damage this mentality can cause in someone's life. Can you imagine inviting someone into a marriage where they will only accept you if you admit your need for them to be worth loving? It is emotional abuse at best and spiritual abuse at worst.

If a friend were in a relationship like this, you would not tell them to stay. This is why the relevance of our sin regarding our relational equity with God diminishes throughout the New Testament. This is why the world is seeing the significance of Jesus in our culture dissipate into nothingness. If we, as Christians, cannot produce answers to the world's questions, but continue to fob off someone's need to understand the pains of life with a statement like, "Well, God is sovereign," then we will become irrelevant to the world.. We need to embrace our questioning. This will help us realise that God himself intends to reveal secrets to us as His beloved children. This will help us present to the world a gospel that makes more sense.

As the church, the body of Christ, we have been the unwilling partners in a false religious expression. In some cases we have been using scripture to control the masses and keep them in the 'fear of God'. In this system we are able to make sure people keep tithing in our churches and stacking our chairs. We don't do this intentionally; for the most part, it has been a learned behaviour founded on a view of a God that we fear instead of one that we love. This is not good news, friends, and it's time we admit it and take responsibility for it.

Church, we have dangled the carrot of heaven for far too long. It has been used as a way to bend the fear we have of death and the hope we hold in Heaven toward our goal of building our congregations. Even on a subconscious level this reality is controlling and abusive. I believe that both Heaven and Hell are products of a choice we make. The Father does not send anyone to heaven or hell; we either choose the relationship and live in the benefits of all that comes with it, or we don't, and face the consequence of living outside of love. Jesus sends us a divine invitation to partake in freedom that comes from all He has done for us.

He never intended His life to become a constant reminder of our shortcomings.

I have left this chapter until the end of this book because you need to read this knowing my heart. I have made a conscious effort on my journey to address the pain I have seen expressed from a christian generation that is deeply wounded by a misrepresentation of God's character. I have decided to take responsibility, where I can, to address these pains instead of ignoring the damage that this has caused many people.

In a moment, I will present to you a God who invites you into belonging so that He can show you how to believe. He accepts you without change and restores you with no strings attached. This is the God I serve. As I have explained in previous chapters, this is not a license to sin. Instead, I am presenting here an invitation to a conversation with God that will allow you to trust Him profoundly and fall in love with Him relentlessly. This is all so that He can begin to transform you from a place outside of your need to be accepted.

Back to the story!

At the end of my conversation with this young man, I remember him saying, "Well, I'm not going to join today." He was a little anxious and shaken up, and the evangelist in me was peaking as I fought with the idea of allowing him to walk away, even though I knew our conversation had impacted him.

The intense emotions I was feeling at this moment were in contradiction to one another. I felt sorrow, because I knew he needed and wanted more, and I felt joy because I knew I had planted something in him that would brood on his heart. A great friend of mine has taught me this truth:

> *"In Genesis 1, the spirit hovers over what? Chaos. What we see standing before us and what is happening in them are two very different things."*
>
> *- Gary Morgan -*

What we often judge before us looks like the chaos we see presented in a life full of brokenness, but we need to understand that this is where the Holy Spirit broods in creation for change. We can jump the gun and stunt the work of the Holy Spirit if we don't allow ourselves to be guided by His wisdom through the art of evangelism.

We don't always get the blessing of seeing the seeds that we plant germinate and become steadfast trees, but now and then, we get to watch God show off with a divine transformation that woos us into a deeper romance. For example seven years ago, I got a phone call from a friend about someone who needed to talk about faith. Unfortunately, they couldn't make it to this person's aid, so I was asked to step in. I had a conversation with the young man about his heart and journey throughout this time, but he was largely unreceptive.

Recently I received a message from him thanking me for our conversation seven years prior. It read like this:

Mate, it has only taken seven years since our chat, but I have found my faith. I am oh so very proud to say I got saved tonight! I am born again, dude! I hope all is well on your end; much love and God bless.

His faith will be much more robust in knowing that he found it with God and not through force-feeding him my version of what he needed to get his life back on track!

Back to the story in the gym. On this day, I got to see God move expediently. When I used Jesus' restoration model instead of mine (in repentance based on our own self-loathing), it became attractive to the listener.

1 Corinthians 3:6 -7

I planted, Apollo's watered, but God gave the growth. So neither he who plants nor he who waters is anything, but only God who gives the growth.

We sometimes stand in the way of what the spirit wants to do in someone's life. On this day, God was going to show me why listening to Him and trusting his process was always a good idea.

Five minutes went past, and I was sharing with my colleague about my desire to help this guy (using the conversation as evangelism to him, I just couldn't help myself). Suddenly, I saw him walking back towards me, and he came and took a seat by my desk. He explained that he had decided he would join as he felt like I cared about him. Here is the kicker: he then began to ask me why it was that I cared at all.

"Why do you care so much?" he asked with a curious tone in its nature. My response came from deep within me as I gazed at a broken man who had felt some relief in me simply seeing him. "My friend, I serve a God who longs to know you and cares deeply for you, and I can see that you are hurting, which means He is hurting. His name is Jesus, and He wants to help you, and so do I. That is why I care so much."

I will never forget the look he gave me right before he explained that he had been a drug-addicted teen and spent some time in a Christian rehab. I watched him as he mustered up the courage to say, "I have heard about Jesus, but I have never heard about Him like this." I spent the next twenty or so minutes with this guy as he came closer and closer to tears. Again, I didn't invite him to accept Christ as his Lord and Saviour, but I did ask him into a relationship. Later that day, he messaged me on Facebook, and we started a dialogue surrounding a conversation in salvation.

Two days later, he asked me to catch up, so I did. In his car, on the way to our meeting, he had an encounter with the God I had told him about. We spent about an hour while he wept over the freedom from his shame and the experience of love that he had.

Two days after this, he had found a church and decided to get baptised. At his baptism one of his family members responded to an altar call to give his life back to Christ. In just one week, this man and his family's lives were radically moulded into a love culture. I couldn't help myself but ask the Father why? And how did this happen?

You are probably struggling, as I did, to feel okay with the reality that perhaps we have made some serious mistakes in our presentation of God to the world. I have realised that our God is more interested in my restoration of a relationship than a moment of salvation. Salvation is a by-product of His desire to know me, and relationship was the vehicle that got me there.

Let's look at this from a biblical perspective. I have touched on this scripture previously in this book, but it is time we take a deeper look; I do not intend to repeat myself, but I believe this will change our lives if we grasp it.

Matthew 4:19

And he said to them, "Follow me, and I will make you fishers of men." Immediately they left their nets and followed him. And going on from there, he saw two other brothers, James, the son of Zebedee, and John, his brother, in the boat with Zebedee, their Father, mending their nets, and he called them. Immediately they left the ship and their Father and followed him.

They were attracted to something that Jesus had to offer. We need to remember that, at this stage, all they had to go by about the character of Jesus was that he was a teacher, or as they would know it, a rabbi. By this age, Jesus was walking in the rabbinic position of authority where He was eligible to teach others and choose His disciples.

You would be forgiven for feeling that the drastic action of dropping their nets and leaving their father" may be a little hard to comprehend. They left their Father standing there to figure it out on his own. However, for them, they were in this moment, responding to a call and being restored into a social system that had previously rejected them. This was a restoration of their standing in the community. The restorative nature of what Jesus presented to them gave them the courage and strength to follow Him so relentlessly.

He gave them their dignity and self-respect in a culture that told them they were unworthy of the call. Does this sound at all familiar? Somehow, we have made salvation a goal to obtain instead of an invitation to restoration and belonging. Maybe, if we would stop focusing on the failings of the world's way and focus on the value of humanity that lives in it, we as a church would have a stronger voice in our communities. But instead, we have lost our influence, and it is because we have made it all about ourselves and what we need instead of doing it in Jesus' way and serving the needs we see.

While seeking this out in prayer with Papa, He said something quite profound to me. "Adam, the Christian world seeks souls to appease me while I look for my sons who have found me."

The reality to grasp here is this: salvation, or an understanding of what God has done and who He is, was never the goal He had in mind. Instead, the Father wants to know us deeply and intimately. He is far less interested in what we achieve for Him than He is inbeing invited into our innermost parts. The gravity of this reality is expressed in the passages of Matthew seven.

Matthew 7:21 - 23

Not everyone who says to me, 'Lord, Lord,' will enter the kingdom of heaven, but the one who does the will of my Father who is in heaven. On that day, many will say to me, 'Lord, Lord, did we not prophesy in your name, and cast out demons in your name, and do many mighty works in your name?' And then will I declare to them, 'I never knew you; depart from me, you workers of lawlessness.'

"Not everyone who says to me Lord, Lord." This is a provocative statement by Jesus; He challenges a culture of performance to gain pleasure in the Father's sight. Before this passage, He refers to the fruits concerning false prophets; "Are grapes gathered from thornbushes or figs from thistles?" It is as if He is presenting the thought that we need to be careful in believing what they have said about Him.

I truly believe Jesus refers to those who focus on what they can do for Him instead of those who have invited Him into a relationship. He is challenging a model based on the previous covenant.

The law of the previous covenant produced this desire to appease God by their works. "Lord, Lord, did we not do all these things in your name?" Understanding this makes clear the intent of His statement toward them, "I never knew you, depart from me." This sounds incredibly harsh, but in reality, He was making a statement to us all; "Would you invite me to get to know you?" Perhaps we have spent too much time knowing about God instead of being known by God.

Let's drive home this restorative model I am claiming that Jesus presents.

Restoration is a primary concern for the follower of Christ. He has modelled this strongly. We see this in Acts with the jailer. The Holy Spirit rocks up after Paul had been beaten nearly to death and thrown into prison. The ground is shaken, the cells are flung wide open, and everyone's chains are loosened. The jailer was about to end his life, but he heard the voice of a believer, "Do not harm yourself; we are all still here." I will let scripture speak for itself on the impact of the nature of restoration for the jailer.

Acts 16:29

And the jailer called for lights and rushed in, and trembling with fear; he fell before Paul and Silas. Then he brought them out and said, "Sirs, what must I do to be saved?"

They restore him by not escaping. Somehow, Paul sees his freedom as less valuable to him than the jailer's life, and this brings the jailer to his knees as he realises he has been delivered from his impending punishment for allowing the prisoners to escape. The jailer responds to this restoration act with a question, "What must I do to be saved?" He responds to the actions of those in the cells as he realises that they have placed his life as more valuable than their freedom. It could have been that Paul realised in this moment, that God's intention in the cell doors being opened was not for escape. Perhaps it happened because there was an opportunity to change the heart of the man in charge of their captivity. We will never truly know, however there is a great lesson for us all in the actions of Paul.

How often have we taken the opportunity to restore those who have held us captive with their judgments, misconceptions, attitudes, and gossip? Often instead of pursuing God's intention toward those around us, we focus on our own right to express our freedom. This is such a challenging scripture; we can be forgiven for thinking that God shaking the foundations, and opening the prison doors, was an invitation to escape.

However, Paul looked at this as an opportunity to introduce the jailer to the nature of the Father. He waited to show him who they were because of the relationship they had with God. This is a common thread throughout the gospel. The attraction to Jesus from the world's perspective was how He made them feel, not what He said to them, the self sacrificial love He displayed was attractive and powerful. Jesus restored people at any cost, even the price of death.

Let's take a look at the Acts 2 churches, for instance. Again, we see a church that grows exponentially in a few days, but why?

We often talk about the day of Pentecost and the spirit coming into power concerning this growth, but we never really look at the cost of growth to the believer.

Acts 2:42

And they devoted themselves to the apostles' teaching and the fellowship, to the breaking of bread and the prayers. And awe came upon every soul, and many wonders and signs were being done through the apostles. And all who believed were together and had all things in common. And they were selling their possessions and belongings and distributing the proceeds to all, as any had need. And day by day, attending the temple together and breaking bread in their homes, they received their food

> *with glad and generous hearts, praising God and having favour with all the people. And the Lord added to their number day by day those who were being saved.*

The spirit was falling and played a pivotal part in what came next. One of the initial purposes of the spirit falling was to provoke a new way of living that was attractive to those who didn't believe. The cost was a selfless lifestyle encouraged by the spirit. Living with one another, sharing, and all who believed were together and had all things in common. This is a powerfully loving community on display.

The spirit did wonders, yes, but perhaps the greatest miracle we see in this passage is the death of selfish human desire. This kind of death to the flesh can only be brought about in the presence of God, and it will look like loving one another. This was attractive to the world. The very next passage shows us the impact of this kind of living, the number of saved people was added daily. We have successfully made the gospel all about us. Lord save us from our sin, the sin that has led us toward negating the reality of your need to know us and feel understood by us. Help us kill this reality through an abandoning of our self-loathing tendencies.

Even in the garden, restoration was always the Father's plan from the inception of the fall. But, then, we see Him come looking for us! He enquires about our hearts, realises we have forgotten whom He has presented himself to be, clothes us and protects us from the tree of life, and sends us out with a rescue mission in mind.

Restoration is His nature.

Genesis 3:8

And they heard the sound of the Lord God walking in the garden in the cool of the day, and the man and his wife hid from the presence of the Lord God among the trees of the garden.

The key here is to understand that the human condition since the fall has produced the natural default of hiding from the presence of God. We do this because we have deemed ourselves unworthy of His presence in the awareness of our sin. When we don't know God's nature correctly, we perpetuate our seperation by placing the responsibility all at His feet.

This is where the world is in regards to God's character. We need to become more like Jesus, to develop a new message of hope regarding the love of the Father.

I have come to realise that a significant part of the mission of Jesus was to restore a picture of the Father that as people we have forgotten. Just as Adam and Eve in the garden didn't trust His character walking through the garden in pursuit of them, this is what we do when we present the gospel without a true understanding. This notion needs to be at the forefront of our minds. But unfortunately, when we talk about God, people have a fallen stance in their perception of who He is. It is ingrained in us from birth, and it is presented all through the media, that Christians and God himself will only love us if we accept that they are correct and we are wrong. It is heartbreaking.

If you listen closely enough, you will hear the broken heart of our Father crying out, "Where are you?" We need to respond not in hiddenness but in authenticity, transparency, and vulnerability. "Here I am, Lord, naked but desiring your presence."

This is the God the world needs to meet - not the one that we have perceived through our hiddenness and broken lenses, but the one who, against all of our ability to believe we are not worth loving, has pursued us as worth it all to the point of death.

So, my friends, I am presenting this to you in the hope that you will understand that the story of the gospel is not one in which you need to come in repentance and shame to feel loved. But instead, it is the story of a Father who desperately wants to know you in ways you cannot imagine. But, above all else, you are loved, worth it, and nothing in heaven, hell, or on earth can change His desire for you.

Let me pray for you, just one last time!

*Father, would you transform our minds,
not through the idea of wrong perspective or
misunderstanding, but instead through the beautiful
journey we are walking through with you.
Would you help us know that we have permission
to doubt, a reason to question, and a brain to reason
with! But more importantly, Father, would you help
our hearts change and genuinely fall in love with
who you are instead of who we think You are.*

Amen.

www.ingramcontent.com/pod-product-compliance
Lightning Source LLC
Chambersburg PA
CBHW020321010526
44107CB00054B/1926